You'd Better
Believe It

David Petts

About the author

After several years in pastoral ministry Dr David Petts served as Principal of Mattersey Hall Bible College from 1977 to 2004. An international Bible teacher, he emphasises the work of the Holy Spirit in the Christian's life and has been instrumental in leading many into the experience of the Baptism in the Holy Spirit. He continues to teach as a visiting lecturer at Mattersey Hall and conducts seminars and Bible studies in churches, colleges, and universities.

David is an Assemblies of God minister and much of his ministry has been within the world-wide Pentecostal movement. He has served as President of the European Pentecostal Theological Association, as Vice Chairman of the Pentecostal European Fellowship, and as a member of the Executive Committee of the Pentecostal World Fellowship. He is, however, happy to preach in interdenominational gatherings, especially where the congregation is sympathetic to his charismatic emphasis.

He is married to Eileen who has been a strong support to his ministry for over 50 years. Their three children are all married and all actively involved in Christian ministry.

A former Exhibitioner of Brasenose College, Oxford, David's academic achievements include an MA, an MTh, and a PhD in Theology. He is an Honorary Academic Fellow of the University of Wales.

Further information may be obtained from his website:

www.davidpetts.org

PREFACE TO THE SIXTH EDITION

The chapters which form the contents of this book were first written as a series of articles for *Youth Aflame* magazine. After many requests they were then made available in book form under the title *Know the Truth*. In 1991 the book was updated, revised, and enlarged to include questions for study purposes at the end of each chapter. The new title, *You'd Better Believe It!* was also adopted at that time. Subsequent editions have contained further improvements and amendments. The sixth edition is essentially a reprint of the fifth, although the format has been modified somewhat.

Although the series was originally written as an explanation of the Fundamental Truths of Assemblies of God, Christians who have experienced the 'charismatic renewal' have also expressed their appreciation. There is a growing awareness that experience is not enough. The Holy Spirit is seeking to guide God's people into the truth of his Word.

We believe that the Bible is the inspired Word of God. The scriptures are the infallible and all-sufficient rule for faith and practice. If we are led by the Spirit who inspired those scriptures to be written, there will be certain teachings upon which all Spirit-filled Christians should be agreed. We must contend earnestly for the faith that was once and for all time delivered to the saints (Jude 3). We need to know the certainty of the things we have been taught (Luke 1:4). It is upon those certainties that these chapters have been written.

DAVID PETTS

July 2014

Contents

INTRODUCTION 8

The Importance of Doctrine..........8

QUESTIONS 11

CHAPTER ONE..............12

Why We Believe in the Bible 12

QUESTIONS 15

CHAPTER TWO 16

The Nature of God 16

QUESTIONS 22

CHAPTER THREE 24

The Life of Christ........................24

QUESTIONS 30

CHAPTER FOUR 32

His Substitutionary Death...........32

QUESTIONS 36

CHAPTER FIVE..............38

His Bodily Resurrection 38

QUESTIONS 43

CHAPTER SIX 44

His Triumphant Ascension..........44

QUESTIONS 49

CHAPTER SEVEN 50

His Abiding Intercession 50

QUESTIONS 54

CHAPTER EIGHT 55

His Second Coming 55

QUESTIONS 59

CHAPTER NINE 61

The Fall of Man 61

QUESTIONS 66

CHAPTER TEN 67

Saved through Faith 67

QUESTIONS 71

CHAPTER ELEVEN 72

The Blood of Christ 72

QUESTIONS 76

CHAPTER TWELVE 77

The New Birth 77

QUESTIONS 81

CHAPTER THIRTEEN 82

Water Baptism 82

QUESTIONS 91

CHAPTER FOURTEEN 93

Breaking of Bread 93

QUESTIONS 98

CHAPTER FIFTEEN 99

The Baptism with the Holy Spirit..99

QUESTIONS 107

CHAPTER SIXTEEN 108

The Gifts of the Holy Spirit 108

QUESTIONS 112

CHAPTER SEVENTEEN............114

The Gifts of Christ 114

QUESTIONS 119

CHAPTER EIGHTEEN 120

Divine Healing 120

QUESTIONS 125

CHAPTER NINETEEN 126

Holiness 126

QUESTIONS 131

CHAPTER TWENTY 132

Heaven and Hell........................132

QUESTIONS 136

INTRODUCTION

The Importance of Doctrine

Some time ago I was invited to minister at an inter-denominational house-fellowship – a charismatic prayer group. During the course of conversation, one of the participants, a very sincere young woman, made the interesting remark: 'I don't want *doctrine.* I want *God'*.

Her statement undoubtedly reflects the attitude of a great many Christians in the world today, who, tired of the dry deadness of denominational dogma, are thirsting for the living reality of life in the Spirit. However, such an attitude, understandable though it may be, is fundamentally dangerous. Like sailing-boats, we need not only the wind of the Spirit – and we certainly *do* need it – to fill our sails and drive us forward for God, but the weighty keel of sound doctrine to keep our vessel upright on the sea of life.

What we believe is of vital importance. The scriptures were written that we might *know the truth*, and that the truth might set us free (John 8:32). Every genuine experience of the Spirit finds its foundation in the truth of God's word. The Bible is the inspired word of God. It teaches the truth – about God, about man, about life and death, good and evil, heaven and hell. If we want to know the truth about any of the important questions of life, we will find it in the Bible.

Doctrine is important

The word *doctrine* which simply means *teaching* occurs at least 50 times in the New Testament, and the emphasis which the early church placed upon it is seen from the many references to Jesus and the apostles *teaching* as well as preaching the word (e.g. Matthew 4:23). When the 3,000 converts on the Day of Pentecost had repented, been baptised, and received the gift of the Holy Spirit, the apostles knew that their first need was to be *taught,* and so these new converts 'devoted themselves to the apostles' teaching' (Acts 2:42). In fact, so important was teaching considered to be that maintaining one's spiritual experience was dependent on continuing in sound teaching:

Anyone who… does not continue in the teaching of Christ, does not have God. Whoever continues in the teaching has both the Father and the Son (2 John 9).

How important teaching is then. It affects our spiritual position before God!

Sources of doctrine

This relationship between our spiritual condition and the doctrine we hold is made clearer when we come to consider what the Bible teaches about sources of doctrine. It is quite possible, for example, for a teaching to be *satanic* in origin. 1 Timothy 4:1 talks about *things taught by demons* and it is clear that the teachings of Spiritualists, Satanists, and others fall into this category.

But not all false doctrine is directly inspired by Satan. Some teachings are said to be of *human* origin. Jesus told his disciples to beware of the teachings of the Pharisees (Matthew 16:12) and said that their teachings were just rules made by men (Matthew 15:9), and Paul warns us of the same danger in Colossians 2:22.

What a wonderful contrast is *the teaching of God our Saviour* (Titus 2:10) which is to be recognised by a right attitude to Christ (2 John 7-10) and a right attitude to scripture (2 Timothy 3:16).

The effects of doctrine

We see then that a doctrine may have its origin in God, in man, or in the devil. Clearly, sound teaching is that which comes from God and false teaching is that which is either human or satanic. But what are the effects of these doctrines upon the people who hold them? We have already noticed that the teachings a person believes may well affect his or her spiritual condition. The effects of doctrine with regard to the person of

Christ are so far-reaching that they determine a person's eternal destiny (2 John 9).

But just as false teaching will lead a person into error, so, thank God, will sound teaching lead into truth. We need to know *what* we believe and *why* we believe it so that we can *by sound doctrine convince those who contradict us* (Titus 1:9). It is by knowing the truth that people are set free (John 8:32).

Doctrine is important. It is vital. We cannot afford to be uninterested. We need to read out Bibles. We need to listen regularly to those whom Christ has set in the Church as teachers (Ephesians 4:11). Timothy was still young when he was told:

Devote yourself to... teaching. Watch your life and doctrine closely; persevere in them; because if you do you will save both yourself and your hearers (1 Timothy 4:13, 16).

QUESTIONS

The questions at the end of each chapter are, of course, entirely optional. The answers are to be found in the verses of the Bible mentioned in the question. If the book is being studied in home groups, the leader may also suggest the right answers.

1. READ John 8:32. Give two reasons why God has given us his word.
2. READ Matthew 4:23. What did Jesus do in addition to preaching?
3. READ Acts 2:41-42. What is placed first in this list of provisions made for young converts?
4. READ 1 Timothy 4:1. What source of doctrine is found here?
5. READ Matthew 16:12, Colossians 2:22. What is the source of doctrine found in these scriptures?
6. READ 2 John 7-10, 2 Timothy 3:16. We recognise right doctrine by two attitudes. What are they?
7. READ Titus 1:9. For what purpose do we need to know what we believe and why we believe it?

CHAPTER ONE

Why We Believe in the Bible

In the brief introduction to this book I pointed out why what we believe is of vital importance; but it is equally important that we should know *why* we believe it. Many Christians today will tell us that they believe the Bible, but sadly comparatively few can tell us why. And yet we are told that we should always be ready to give a reason for the things we believe (1 Peter 3:15). If the Bible is the basis of all that we believe, it is important that we should know why we believe it!

The Bible itself claims to be inspired

In 2 Timothy 3:16 we read that *All scripture is God-breathed* (inspired by God) and 2 Peter 1:21 tells us that:

Prophecy never had its origin in the will of man, but men spoke from God as they were carried along by the Holy Spirit.

What was written in the scriptures was considered to have come, not from man, but from God himself.

But in fact the Bible claims even more than this. It claims not only to be inspired by God, but also to be all that we need. It is all-sufficient. It tells us all we need to know. Deuteronomy 29:29 tells us:

The secret things belong to the Lord our God; but the things revealed belong to us and our children forever, that we may follow all the words of this law.

All we need to know is *the things revealed.* This principle is true *for ever* and the things revealed are *all the words of this law.* Any teaching that is not found to be clearly taught in the Bible is to be rejected. The Bible alone is the inspired word of God. It is all that we need for faith and practice.

Jesus believed the Bible was inspired

There are, of course, those who would say that to accept the Bible's testimony of itself is unfair. They tell us that they are Christians because they believe in Jesus, but they are not prepared to accept that the Bible itself is true. Such people, however, have clearly never examined what Jesus himself taught about the Bible.

With regard to the Old Testament, Jesus stated that *the scripture cannot be broken* (John 10:35). The Sadducees were in error because they were ignorant of the scriptures (Mark 12:24). It was *easier for heaven and earth to disappear than for the least stroke of a pen to drop out of the law* (Luke 16:17). As far as Jesus was concerned, when the Bible spoke, *God* spoke. In Genesis 2:24 the scripture states that a man shall leave father and mother and take a wife. In Matthew 19:4-5 Jesus says that *God* said this. It is surely enough for us, as Jesus' disciples, to believe as he believed.

The New Testament, of course, had not been written at the time of Christ. But Jesus promised his disciples that the Holy Spirit would accurately remind them of his teachings and would lead them into further truth for which they were not yet ready. The Spirit would teach them *all* things, remind them of *all* the truth (John 14:26, 16:12-13). Christians should believe the Bible if for no other reason than that Jesus himself claimed it to be inspired by God.

The apostles taught that the Bible was inspired

As we read the New Testament we discover that the writers were aware of the inspiration that Jesus had promised. Their writings were not a product of their own wisdom or ability. They were conscious of direct guidance and authority from God. The things they wrote were *the commandments of the Lord* taught directly by the Holy Spirit (1 Corinthians 2:13, 14:37) and their writings were acknowledged as equal to those of the Old Testament.

Notice how, in 1 Timothy 5:18, Paul quotes Matthew (NT) alongside Deuteronomy (OT) and evidently considers both as an integral part of 'scripture':

For the scripture says, Do not muzzle the ox while it is treading out the grain (Deuteronomy 25:4) and, The worker deserves his wages (Matthew 10:10).

The same attitude is adopted by Peter in 2 Peter 3:15-16, when he refers to Paul's letters as part of 'the scriptures'.

It is clear then that the three major sources of Christian teaching available to us – the Bible, the early church, and Jesus himself – all declare that the Bible is the inspired word of God. So-called Christians who question the authority of the Bible make nonsense of Christianity, for if the Bible is wrong, then Jesus was wrong in believing it. To reject the Bible is to reject Christianity.

Christian experience confirms that the Bible is inspired

There is, however, one final evidence of the Bible's authority. The Bible is not merely a textbook for Christian doctrine. It is a guidebook for life – a handbook for Christian living. The Bible is proved true by the fact that when we put it into practice, it works. Its promises are fulfilled when we meet the conditions. Prayers are answered. Lives are changed. The sick are healed. Millions have found from their own experience that the Bible is wonderfully true. The Bible *is* the inspired word of God. If you want to be sure, test it, and see for yourself!

QUESTIONS

1. READ 1 Peter 3:15. What should we always be prepared to do?

2. READ 2 Timothy 3:16, 2 Peter 1:21. Who inspired the Bible to be written?

3. READ Deuteronomy 29:29. Where has God revealed to us the things we need to know?

4. READ Mark 12:24, John 10:35. What did Jesus say about scripture in these verses?

5. Jesus accepted the Old Testament stories and miracles as fact. Which ones are mentioned in the following scriptures?

    Matthew 12:3-4

    Matthew 12:40

    Matthew 19:4-5

    Luke 4:26

    Luke 4:27

    Luke 17:27

    Luke 17:29

    John 3:14

6. READ Luke 24:27. How did Jesus use the scriptures here?

7. READ 1 Corinthians 2:13. Who does Paul say taught him?

8. READ 1 Corinthians 14:37. What were the things Paul wrote?

9. Can you remember any instances in your life and experience that illustrate:

    A promise fulfilled when the conditions were met?

    Prayer answered?

    A life changed?

    A sick person healed?

CHAPTER TWO

The Nature of God

Although the leaders of the various world religions have attempted in their own way to show their followers what God is like, their efforts have, of necessity, failed. It is quite impossible for any human being to understand the nature of God, apart from what God in his mercy has chosen to reveal to us.

As Christians we believe that God reveals himself to us in a variety of ways. We know something about him from the beauty of the world around us, which leaves us with no excuse for doubting his existence (Romans 1:19-21). But it is in the person of his Son and through the revelation of his word that we discover what God is truly like, and as we examine the word of God we find that although there is only *one* true God, he is, nevertheless, revealed in *three* persons.

It is, of course, extremely difficult for our minds to understand how God can be 'one being in three persons', but we do well to remember that our limited, human minds can never expect to understand the infinite. We should content ourselves to see that this is what he has revealed himself to be in holy scripture, and remember that a god who is capable of being fully understood by our little minds could hardly be God at all! What then does the Bible teach us about God?

God is One

Both Old and New Testaments emphatically declare that there is only one God:

Hear, O Israel, the Lord our God, the Lord is one (Deuteronomy 6:4).

See now that I am he. There is no god besides me (Deuteronomy 32:39).

You alone are God (Psalm 86:10).

I am the first and I am the last. Apart from me there is no god (Isaiah 44:6).

I am the Lord and there is no other; apart from me there is no god (Isaiah 45:5-6).

There is no God but one... There is but one God, the father from whom all things come (1 Corinthians 8:4, 6).

It is important to realise, however, that the main emphasis of *all* these verses is to contrast the God of Israel with the idol gods of the nations. What is being taught is not so much that the Lord is one person, as the fact that he is the *only* true God. He is the *one* true and living God (as distinct from the *many* false and lifeless idols). However, as the New Testament makes clear, the one true and living God has revealed himself to us in three persons, Father, Son, and Holy Spirit.

God is Three

Those who have not fully understood what Christians believe in this respect have claimed that we believe in three gods. (This was in fact one of Mohammed's main criticisms of Christianity, though he mistakenly believed that Christians taught that the virgin Mary was one of the Trinity!) The Bible, however, does not teach that there are three gods, but that there is *one* God revealed in *three* persons.

There are many verses in the New Testament that show us that there are three distinct persons each of whom is God:

He saw the **Spirit of God** *(the Holy Spirit) descending like a dove, and lighting upon* **him** *(Jesus, God the Son), and a* **voice from heaven** *(God the Father's) said, This is my Son* (Matthew 3:16-17).

I (God the Son) will ask the **Father** *(God the Father) and he will give you* **another counsellor** *(God the Holy Spirit) (John 14:16).*

Therefore go and make disciples of all nations, baptising them in the name of the **Father** *and of the* **Son,** *and of the* **Holy Spirit** (Matthew 28:19).

*Exalted to the right hand of God, **he** (Jesus, God the Son) has received from **the Father** the promised **Holy Spirit** (Acts 2:33).*

God (the Father) anointed Jesus of Nazareth (God the Son) with the Holy Spirit (Acts 10:38).

***Christ** (God the Son), who through the eternal **Spirit** offered himself unblemished to **God** (the Father) (Hebrews 9:14).*

*The grace of **the Lord Jesus Christ** (God the Son), and the love of **God** (the Father), and the fellowship of the **Holy Spirit** be with you all (2 Corinthians 13:14).*

We see from these verses that the Son and the Spirit are *distinct from* and yet mentioned *along with* the Father. They are clearly all separate persons, but are they all God? Before we can answer this adequately, we must answer the question, *What is God like?*

What is God like?

The Bible tells us a great deal about God and it is clear that there are certain attributes (or qualities) which are given to God alone. No one else possesses these qualities. If God did not have them, he would not be God. For anyone else to have them would mean that they too were God! The qualities are sometimes referred to as *attributes of deity*, and although there are others, for the purpose of our discussion we shall mention just five.

The Bible shows us that God is:

Creator	Genesis 1:1
Omnipotent	Matthew 19:26, Job 42:2
Omnipresent	Jeremiah 23:24
Omniscient	1 John 3:20
Eternal	Psalm 90:2

In other words, God made everything, can do anything, is everywhere, knows everything, always has been and always will be!

As we have already said, *anyone* who possesses these attributes must be God, for God alone possesses them. But what we must now ask ourselves is, *Does Jesus possess these attributes? Is **he** God? Does the Holy Spirit possess these attributes? Is **he** God?* And if the Bible answers *yes* to these questions, we will have shown that, although there is only one God, he is nevertheless revealed in three persons – Father, Son, and Holy Spirit.

There are of course those who deny this doctrine. The 'Jehovah's Witnesses' for example tell us that Jesus is not God and that the Holy Spirit, although divine, is not a person. In the remainder of this chapter we shall seek to answer these objections and to demonstrate that the Holy Spirit is a divine person and that Jesus is not only *the Son of God* but also *God the Son.*

Is the Holy Spirit a person?

Nowhere in the Bible do we find the words, *The Holy Spirit is a person.* But neither does the Bible tell us that *Jesus is a person* in so many words. Yet no intelligent person can possibly read the Bible and doubt the personality of the Lord Jesus Christ, because although the Bible does not actually say so, it is obvious from what we read about him that he was (and is) a person!

And the same is true of the Holy Spirit. The Bible makes it quite clear that he possesses personal attributes and engages in personal activities. The Holy Spirit has a mind (Romans 8:27) and he has a will (1 Corinthians 12:11). He may be grieved (Ephesians 4:30, Isaiah 63:10). He teaches, testifies, reproves, guides, speaks, hears and shows (John 14:26, 15:26, 16:13).

These verses show conclusively that the Holy Spirit is not a mere impersonal force, for only a person can hear or speak etc. Other verses which might be quoted are Acts 9:31, 13:2, 16:6, Romans 8:16, 26, 15:16, and 1 Corinthians 2:10.

The Holy Spirit, then, is a person. But is he God?

Is the Holy Spirit God?

As we have already seen, there are certain attributes or qualities that are possessed by God alone. God is creator, omnipotent, omnipresent, omniscient, eternal. If we can show that the Bible teaches that the Holy Spirit possesses these attributes, we will have shown that the Holy Spirit is God.

The second verse of the Bible shows us the work of the Holy Spirit in creation and Job 33:4 plainly states *The Spirit of the Lord has made me.* His omnipotence is shown in Luke 1:35-37 where we read, *The Holy Spirit will come upon you... for nothing shall be impossible with God.* The Psalmist asks *Where can I go from your Spirit* (Psalm 139:7), revealing the omnipresence of the Spirit. His omniscience is seen in such passages as 1 Corinthians 2:10 and Acts 5:3-4: *How is it that you have you lied to the Holy Spirit? ... You have not lied to men but to God.* And Hebrews 9:14 describes him as the *eternal Spirit.* The Holy Spirit, therefore, is the eternal, omnipotent, omniscient, omnipresent creator. He is God.

Is Jesus God?

And what is true of the Holy Spirit is also true of our Lord Jesus Christ; for the Bible clearly shows us that Jesus possesses all the divine attributes. Jesus is creator, for John 1:3 declares that all things were made by him. Similarly Paul tells us that:

By him all things were created, things in heaven and on earth, visible and invisible, whether thrones or powers or rulers or authorities; all things were created by him and for him (Colossians 1:16).

As creator, Jesus is omnipotent. He is *the mighty God* (Isaiah 9:6) and all power is given to him (Matthew 28:18). He is omnipresent, for *where two or three come together* in his name, there *he is with them* (Matthew 18:20). He is omniscient because he knows all things (John 21:17).

He is eternal, for he is *the same yesterday, today and forever* (Hebrews 13:8). He is the *everlasting father* (Isaiah 9:6). He is with us always (Matthew 28:20). His *goings forth have been from the days of eternity* (Micah 5:2 footnote). He is the word who was in the beginning (John1:1). He existed before Abraham was (John 8:58). He *is the Alpha and Omega, who is and who was and who is to come, the Almighty* (Revelation 1:8), *the first and the last... alive for ever and ever* (Revelation 1:17-18).

But the testimony to the deity of Christ is stronger still. He is equal with God (Philippians 2:6). Anyone who has seen him has seen the Father (John 14:9). He is *God with us* (Matthew 1:23). He is our great God and saviour (Titus 2:13). No wonder we read that people worshipped him! (Matthew 14:33, 28:9, 17, Luke 24:52, John 9:38). God demands that Jesus be worshipped: *Let all the angels worship him* (Hebrews 1:6). Indeed, God himself declares Jesus to be God:

To the Son he says, Your throne, O God, will last for ever and ever (Hebrews 1:8).

No wonder that with Thomas (John 20:28) we exclaim, *My Lord and my God!*

What is God like? We see him in Jesus.

QUESTIONS

1. Both Old and New Testaments emphatically declare that there is only one God. Which words in the following scriptures show this?

   Deuteronomy 6:4

   Deuteronomy 32:39

   Psalm 86:10

   Isaiah 44:6

   Isaiah 45:5, 6

   1 Corinthians 8:4, 6

2. READ Romans 1:19-21. In what way has God spoken to us here?

3. In the following scriptures write out the words that refer to one of the persons of the Godhead. There may be more than one person referred to in each scripture.

   Matthew 3:16-17

   Matthew 18:19

   John 14:16

   Acts 2:33

   Acts 10:38

   Hebrews 9:14

   2 Corinthians 13:14

4. What quality of God is referred to in the following verses?

   Genesis 1:1

   Job 42:2 and Matthew 19:26

   Jeremiah 23:24

   1 John 3:20

   Psalm 90:2

5. In the following scriptures, what words show conclusively that the Holy Spirit is not a mere impersonal force, but that he possesses personal attributes and engages in personal activities?

Romans 8:27

1 Corinthians 12:11

Ephesians 4:30

Isaiah 63:10

Genesis 6:3

John 14:26

John 15:26

John 16:8

John 16:13

6. What words in the following scriptures show that the Holy Spirit possesses each of the attributes of God?

Genesis 1:1-2, Job 33:4

Luke 1:35-37

Psalm 139:7

1 Corinthians 2:10, Acts 5:3-4

Hebrews 9:14

7. What words in the following scriptures show that Jesus possesses divine attributes?

John 1:3, Colossians 1:16

Isaiah 9:6, Matthew 28:18

Matthew 18:20

John 21:17

Hebrews 13:8, Isaiah 9:6, Matthew 28:20, Micah 5:2, John 1:1, John 8:58, Revelation 1:8 and 1:17-18

8. READ Philippians 2:6. With whom is Jesus equal?

9. READ John 14:9. Who have we seen if we have seen Jesus?

10. READ Matthew 1:23. What name or title is given to Jesus?

11. READ Hebrews 1:6 and 8. How do these verses show that Jesus is God?

CHAPTER THREE

The Life of Christ

In the introductory chapter we considered the importance of knowing what we believe and why we believe it. Then we saw why it is reasonable to believe that the Bible is the inspired word of God. In the last chapter we examined the nature of God and saw that he has revealed himself as *one being in three persons – Father, Son, and Holy Spirit.* We now turn our attention to the birth, life and ministry of our Lord Jesus Christ, God the Son, who *became flesh and lived for a while among us* (John 1:14).

His virgin birth

The Bible teaches that the entry of Jesus Christ into this world was quite different from that of any other human being, for in his conception and birth, as well as in his life and death, he is unique among men.

Despite the arguments of those who refuse to believe God's word, those who accept the authority of scripture will find no difficulty in accepting the plain biblical teaching of the virgin birth. The prophet Isaiah declared that a virgin would conceive and would bear a son whose name would be Immanuel (Isaiah 7:14). The Holy Spirit tells us in Matthew 1:23 that this prophecy was fulfilled at the birth of Christ, and although some translate the word *virgin* as *young woman*, it is quite clear from the passages in Matthew and Luke that the word is to be taken literally.

Mary herself could not understand how she could possibly bear a child, for as she herself declared, *I am a virgin* (Luke 1:34). To this the angel replied that the Holy Spirit would come upon her and that therefore her child would be the Son of God (Luke 1:35). Matthew 1:18 clearly states that Mary was with child *through the Holy Spirit* before Mary and Joseph *came together* and in verse 25 Joseph *had no union with her until she gave birth to a son.*

It is interesting to notice, incidentally, that Mary did not remain a virgin, as some teach. This verse makes it quite clear that after the birth of Jesus Mary and Joseph lived a normal married life and that Mary had other children. Mark 6:3 confirms that Jesus had brothers and sisters and names James, Joses, Juda and Simon. These other children were conceived in the normal way, having Mary as their mother and Joseph as their father.

Jesus, however, was the Son of God and was conceived of the Holy Spirit and born of the virgin Mary. This is not only perfectly reasonable, for *with God all things are possible,* but it is also completely logical, for how else could Jesus be both *Son of God* and *Son of Man?* He was *born of a woman* (Galatians 4:4) but he is the *man from heaven* (1 Corinthians 15:47). By his miraculous conception Christ partook of human nature without receiving the corruption of human nature. He was the last Adam who succeeded where Adam failed.

His sinless life

The purpose of the coming of the Lord Jesus Christ was that he might save sinners (1 Timothy 1:15). To do so he must be able to offer a perfect sacrifice for sin. He was to be the *lamb of God who takes away the sin of the world* (John 1:29) and the lamb must be *without defect* (Exodus 12:5, Leviticus 9:3, 14:10). To bring the unrighteous to God, he himself must be righteous (1 Peter 3:18). It is by his righteousness and obedience that we are made righteous (Romans 5:18-19). If Jesus had not lived a sinless life he could not have saved us from our sin.

But, thank God, he was sinless. He had no sin (2 Corinthians 5:21). He did no sin (1 Peter 2:22). He was tempted in every way just as we are and yet without sin (Hebrews 4:15). He is holy, blameless, pure and set apart from sinners (Hebrews 7:26). For this reason he is able to offer himself 'without defect' to God on our behalf, and because he never yielded to temptation and was always victorious over sin, he knows how to help us when we are tempted (Hebrews 2:18). By his sinless life he was able to offer a perfect sacrifice for sin. The sinless one bore our sins in his body on the cross in order that we might be free from sin's penalty and free from sin's power.

His miraculous ministry

Yes, Jesus was unique: in parentage, for God was his Father; in purity, for his life was sinless; in power, for there was never a man like Jesus! Even the briefest glimpse at the Gospels is sufficient to show that Jesus was no ordinary man! The table below is just a brief summary of the vast scope of Jesus' miraculous power. It may prove useful for reference purposes.

THE SCOPE OF HIS MIRACULOUS POWER

Power over disease

The blind	Matthew 9:27-31, 20:29-34
	Mark 8:22-26, 10:46-52
	Luke 18:35-42
	John 9:1-7
The deaf and mute	Mark 7:31-37
The lepers	Matthew 8:1-4, Mark 1:40-45
	Luke 5:12-16, 17:11-19
The paralysed	Matthew 8:5-13, 9:1-8
	Mark 2:1-12
	Luke 5:17-26, 7:1-10
	John 5:1-9
The deformed	Matthew 12:9-14
	Mark 3:1-6
	Luke 6:6-11
Fever	Matthew 8:14-17
	Mark 1:29-31

	Luke 4:38-39
Internal Haemorrhage	Matthew 9:20-22
	Mark 5:25-34
	Luke 8:43-48
The wounded	Luke 22:50-51
At a distance	Matthew 8:5-13
	Luke 7:1-10
	John 4:46-54
All kinds of sickness	Matthew 4:23-24, 8:16, 9:35
	Mark 6:56
	Luke 6:17-19

Power over demons

Dumb demon	Matthew 9:32-34
Blind & dumb demon	Matthew 12:22-32
	Luke 11:14-23
Unclean spirit	Mark 1:21-28
	Luke 4:31-37
Legion	Matthew 8:28-34
	Mark 5:1-20
	Luke 8:26-33
Boy	Matthew 17:14-20
	Mark 9:14-19
	Luke 9:37-43
Syro-Phoenician's daughter	Matthew 15: 21-28
	Mark 7:24-30

Power over nature

Water into wine	John 2:1-11
Feeding the 4,000	Matthew 15:32-39
	Mark 8:1-10
Feeding the 5,000	Matthew 14:13-21
	Mark 6:30-44
	Luke 9:10-17
	John 6:1-14
Fig tree withered	Matthew 21:18-22
	Mark 11:12-14
Stilling the storm	Matthew 8:23-27
	Luke 8:22-25
Walking on water	Matthew 14:22-27
	Mark 6:45-52
	John 6:16-21

Power over death

Jairus' daughter	Matthew 9:23-26
	Mark 5:35-43
	Luke 8:40-56
Widow of Nain's son	Luke 7:11-17
Lazarus	John 11:1-44

THE PURPOSE OF HIS MIRACLES

To deliver from danger	Matthew 8:23-27
To provide for those in need	Matthew 14:13-21
	John 2:1-11
To teach a lesson on faith	Matthew 21:18-22
To destroy the works of	Acts 10:38

the devil	1 John 3:8
To demonstrate God's love	Matthew 14:14
To prove who he was	Matthew 11:2-5
	John 5:36
To convince those in doubt	John 14:11
To draw people to himself	John 6:2
To bring glory to God	Matthew 15:30-31

After such a catalogue of mighty works we find it impossible to believe that anyone who takes the Gospels seriously can seriously doubt the miraculous ministry of the Lord Jesus Christ. Remove the miraculous from the Gospels and there is little left! Indeed to remove the miraculous is to remove Christianity, for our faith is founded on the greatest miracle of all – the resurrection of our Lord Jesus Christ, and without *that* our faith is pointless (1 Corinthians 15:17).

But Christ *is* alive. The proof of his miraculous ministry lies not only in the historical evidence of the Gospels themselves, but in the living experience of millions who have discovered in our own day and generation that he still works miracles for those who believe in his name (John 14:12, Mark 16:16-18).

QUESTIONS

1. READ Isaiah 7:14.

   Who did Isaiah say would conceive?

   What would be the name of the child?

   When and how was this prophecy fulfilled? (See Matthew 1:23)

2. READ Luke 1:31-35

   Why was Mary puzzled?

   Whose child did the angel say the child would be?

3. READ Matthew 1:18, 25

   From whom was the child conceived?

4. READ I Timothy 1:15.

   For what purposes did our Lord Jesus Christ come into the world?

5. What words in the following scriptures show us that Jesus was sinless?

   2 Corinthians 5:21

   1 Peter 2:22

   Hebrews 4:15

   Hebrews 7:26

6. In each of the following scriptures, what do you think was the purpose of the miracle?

    Matthew 8:23-27

    Matthew 14:13-21, John 2:1-11

    Matthew 21:18-22

    Acts 10:38, 1 John 3:8

    Matthew 14:14

    Matthew 11:2-5

    John 14:11

    John 6:2

    Matthew 15:30-31

7. Do you know of any recent miracles which show that God's power and purposes are still the same?

CHAPTER FOUR

His Substitutionary Death

In the last chapter we examined the subject of the life of the Lord Jesus. Now we must consider the importance of his death. It is interesting to notice that although the life of our Lord here on earth lasted for more than 30 years, it is on the *week* of his *death* that the Gospel writers focus their attention. Of the 89 chapters of the Gospels, no fewer than 30 (i.e. over one third) centre around the death of Christ. In fact, the cross is central not only to the New Testament, but to the whole Bible. The Old Testament looks forward to it. The New Testament looks back. The gospel by which we are saved is that *Christ died for our sins according to the scriptures* (1 Corinthians 15:1-4).

When we refer to Christ's death on the cross for our sins, we sometimes use the word *atonement.* We believe in the substitutionary, atoning death of the Lord Jesus Christ, and it is the importance of the atonement that we shall be considering in this chapter.

The meaning of atonement

The word *atonement* is best understood if we break it into three parts: *at-one-ment.* This is the root Anglo-Saxon meaning of the word. To atone is to make at one. The death of Christ is an atoning death because it makes sinners *at one* with God.

The need for atonement

The Bible teaches that it is our sins that have separated us from God (Isaiah 59:1-2). We can only be brought back to God if our sins are dealt with. No one is excluded from this, for *all have sinned and fall short of the glory of God* (Romans 3:23). Again and again the Bible makes this clear. *There is no one who does not sin* (1 Kings 8:46). *There is no one who does good, no not one* (Psalm 14:3). *There is not a righteous man on the earth who does what is right and never sins*

(Ecclesiastes 7:20). *No one is good except God* (Mark 10:18). *If we claim to be without sin, we deceive ourselves* (1 John 1:8). No wonder Paul could say, *The whole world is a prisoner to sin* (Galatians 3:22).

But the Bible does not only teach us that all have sinned. It warns us of the seriousness of sin. Sin is an offence to God who is holy. His eyes are too pure to look on evil (Habakkuk 1:13). He simply will not tolerate sin. Consequently sin separates us from God. *Our sins have hidden his face from us* (Isaiah 59:2) for *The Lord is far from the wicked* (Proverbs 15:29).

Unless our sins are dealt with, our separation from God will be eternal. Jesus himself talked about hell fire (Matthew 5:22), outer darkness (Matthew 8:12), and eternal punishment (Matthew 25:46). Paul tells us that the wages of sin is death (Romans 6:23) and that the wrath of God is coming (Colossians 3:6).

The Lord Jesus will be revealed from heaven in blazing fire with his powerful angels. He will punish those who do not know God and do not obey the gospel of our Lord Jesus Christ. They will be punished with everlasting destruction, and shut out from the presence of the Lord and from the majesty of his power (2 Thessalonians 1:7-9).

Sin is serious. It separates from God. There is nothing we can do about it. We cannot hide it, for our sin will find us out (Numbers 32:23). We cannot cleanse ourselves from it. We cannot even make up for it by trying to do good. This is the fundamental mistake so many make, but the scriptures clearly tell us that no one can be righteous in God's sight by keeping the law (Romans 3:20, Galatians 2:16). We have all sinned. We are all separated from God. There is nothing we can do. We all need a Saviour.

The means of atonement

When God first revealed to man the need for atonement, he made the means of atonement quite clear. *It is the blood that makes atonement* (Leviticus 17:11). This is not just an Old Testament principle. It is carried over into the New. It is eternally valid. *Without the shedding of blood there is no forgiveness* (Hebrews 9:22). And this is why Christ died. This is why he shed his blood. He made peace through the blood of his cross in order to reconcile us sinners to God (Colossians 1:20). He did this by offering himself as a sacrifice to God (Ephesians 5:2). He is the Lamb of God who takes away the sin of the world (John 1:29). This was the purpose of his death. He bore our sins in his own body on the cross (1 Peter 2:24).

But his death was not only sacrificial. It was also substitutionary. Christ died *for* us. His death counts as our death. He died in our place. Because of our sin, *we* should die. Instead, *Christ* has died for us. He was wounded for our transgressions (Isaiah 53:5). He suffered for sins, the righteous for the unrighteous, to bring us to God (1 Peter 3:18). We deserved to die because of our sin, but because he loved us, he came and died in our place, as our substitute, that we might live. All that he requires of us is that we repent and believe.

The results of the atonement

By his atoning death upon the cross of Calvary, Jesus has made the way open for every sinner to come to God. He died for all. He has no favourites. There is no respect of persons with God. *Whoever* shall call on the name of the Lord shall be saved. The offer of God's forgiveness is open to all, but it is only received by those who accept it in repentance and faith. Those who will not repent will perish (Luke 13:5), for Jesus is the *only* way of salvation (John 14:6).

But to those who have accepted his offer of mercy amazing privileges are given. Our sins are forgiven. God's wrath is removed. We are no longer his enemies (Romans 5:10). He declares us righteous – looks on us as though we had never sinned at all! Amazing grace! We are adopted into his family.

We already have the rights of sons (Galatians 4:4-7), but there's more to come!

How great is the love the Father has lavished on us, that we should be called children of God! And that is what we are! ... Dear friends, now we are children of God, and what we will be has not yet been made known, but we know that when he appears we shall be like him, for we shall see him as he is! (1 John 3:1-2).

What a glorious destiny! And all because Jesus died for us.

QUESTIONS

1. READ 1 Corinthians 15:1-4. What did Christ do according to the scriptures?

2. READ Isaiah 59:1-2. What has separated us from God?

3. READ Romans 3:23. This tells us that all have sinned. Which words in the following verses also make this clear?

   1 Kings 8:46

   Psalm 14:3

   Ecclesiastes 7:20

   Mark 10:18

   1 John 1:8

4. READ Habakkuk 1:13. What can God not do? Why not?

5. READ Isaiah 59:2. What is the consequence of God not looking at sin?

6. READ Proverbs 15:29. What else does this tell us about God and the sinner?

7. How is separation from God described by Jesus himself in the following scriptures?

   Matthew 5:22

   Matthew 8:12

   Matthew 25:46

8. How does the apostle Paul describe this separation? See:

   Romans 6:23

   Colossians 3:6

   2 Thessalonians 1:7-9.

9. READ Numbers 32:23. Can we cover up our sin?

10. READ Proverbs 20:9. Can we cleanse ourselves from sin?

11. READ Romans 3:20 and Galatians 2:15-16. Can we make up for our sin by doing good?

12. READ Leviticus 17:11.

What is it that makes atonement for our sins?

Is this just an Old Testament principle, or does it carry over into the New? (See Hebrews 9:22).

13. READ Colossians 1:20. What did Christ make through the blood of his cross?

14. READ Ephesians 5:2. How is Jesus' death described here?

15. READ 1 Peter 2:24. Whose sins did Jesus bear?

16. READ Isaiah 53:5 and 1 Peter 3:18. What words show that Jesus died instead of us?

17. If we accept God's offer of mercy, what amazing privileges are ours? See:

1 John 2:2

Romans 5:10

Galatians 4:4-7.

CHAPTER FIVE

His Bodily Resurrection

We have already considered in an earlier chapter why we believe that the Bible is the inspired word of God. Having agreed that this is so, it is hardly necessary to ask the question, *Did Christ rise from the dead?* as the Gospel records make it quite clear that he did. In this chapter, however, we shall attempt to show, even to the person who does not accept the doctrine of the inspiration of scripture, that it is reasonable to believe in the bodily resurrection of the Lord Jesus Christ.

Scriptural evidence

The New Testament teaches that there were at least ten separate occasions on which the Lord Jesus appeared to his disciples in bodily form. The order of events seems to have been as follows:

On the first day

1. To Mary Magdalene (Mark 16:9-11, John 20:11-18)
2. To women returning from the tomb (Matthew 28:8-10)
3. To Peter (Luke 24:34, 1 Corinthians 15:5)
4. To the Emmaus disciples (Luke 24:13-35)
5. To the disciples - Thomas absent (Mark 16:14, Luke 24:33-39, John 20:19-23)

A week later

1. To the disciples – Thomas present (John 20:26-29)

On subsequent occasions

1. To seven disciples at the Sea of Tiberias (John 21:1-23)
2. To the eleven and others on a Galilean mountain (Matthew 28:16-18, 1 Corinthians 15:6)
3. To James (1 Corinthians 15:7)
4. To the eleven (Mark 16:14-19, Luke 24:50-52).

Opponents of Christianity have argued that the accounts in each of the four Gospels are so different that they cannot possibly all be true. However, although the exact order of events as they took place on resurrection morning is difficult to follow, various solutions have been suggested. The Schofield Reference Bible, for example, offers the following explanation:

"Three women, Mary Magdalene, Mary the mother of James and Joses, and Salome, start for the sepulchre, followed by other women bearing spices. The three find the stone rolled away and Mary Magdalene goes to tell the disciples. Salome and Mary the mother of James and Joses draw nearer the tomb and see the angel of the Lord, and go back to meet the women with the spices. Meanwhile, Peter and John, warned by Mary Magdalene of the empty tomb, arrive, look in and go away. Mary Magdalene returns with them, but remains weeping, sees two angels, and then Jesus, and goes as he told her to tell the disciples. Meanwhile, Mary the mother of James and Joses, and Salome have met the women with the spices, and returning with them they see two angels. They also receive the angelic message, and going to seek the disciples are met by Jesus".

This attempt to harmonise the Gospel accounts may or may not be correct, but at least it shows that harmonisation is possible. Whatever we may make of the order of events and appearances, one thing is abundantly plain. The Gospel writers are all agreed that Jesus Christ rose bodily from the dead. But how historical is this evidence as far as the sceptic is concerned?

Historical evidence (apart from the scriptures)

Even for those who do not accept the divine inspiration of the Gospel records, the evidence from the historical standpoint is extremely strong. Those who wish to study this at some length should read *Who Moved the Stone?* by Frank Morison, the story of a man who set out to prove that Christ did *not* rise from the dead, but who, upon examining the evidence, became convinced that he did! A shorter work is the booklet by

Professor J.N.D. Anderson entitled *The Evidence for the Resurrection* in which the author informs us that the New Testament documents *are* reliable. With reference to the resurrection accounts in 1 Corinthians, Mark and Luke, he states that

There is scarcely a scholar who has doubted the genuineness of 1 Corinthians, and its date is generally accepted as about 56AD.

Some modern scholars believe that an Aramaic version (of Mark) *was in existence as early as 44AD.*

Not only have the third Gospel and Acts been widely accepted as the genuine composition of Luke, the beloved physician, but Sir William Ramsay and others have shown us what a minutely accurate historian he was.

We see, then, that the Gospel records are historically as reliable as any others, even when we discount our own view of divine inspiration. What then are the arguments of those who disbelieve and how can we answer them?

Arguments and answers

First, there are those who tell us that the whole story was a deliberate invention. But in 56AD Paul told the Corinthians that the majority of over 500 people who saw the risen Christ were still alive. Were they all deceivers? The Christian faith has given the world the highest moral and ethical teaching it has ever known. Can this have begun with a lie? The suggestion that the story of the resurrection was a deliberate invention on the part of the disciples is utterly unthinkable, as is the equally absurd suggestion that the disciples stole the body. Most of the first disciples were eventually put to death for preaching the resurrection. If they knew it was untrue, why didn't they own up and save their lives?

Then there are those who have suggested that the women mistook the tomb. They went to anoint the body of Jesus, but went to the wrong tomb, and so assumed that he had risen! But if this were so, why did the Jewish priests accuse the disciples of stealing the body? Why did they not simply point out the right tomb?!

Others maintain that Jesus was not really dead. He appeared to die on the cross, but recovered in the tomb and presumably walked out! But could a man who had suffered the agony of crucifixion have survived for three days without food, water, or medical attention and then have been strong enough to move a stone that three women felt unable to tackle, and to walk for miles on nail-pierced feet? It is easier to believe in the resurrection! Besides, this theory also involves Christ in gross deception, which is inconsistent with the character he is described as possessing in the Gospels.

Lastly, there have been those who have suggested that the resurrection was in fact a psychological hallucination. But those who know anything about such phenomena will admit that the resurrection appearances of our Lord cannot be explained in these terms. Only certain types of people are susceptible to hallucination. Were the 500 witnesses all of the same type? Further, it is a recognised fact of psychiatry that two people seldom, if ever, suffer from the same hallucination, and such experiences are usually recurrent over a long period of time (not just for a period of 40 days). And were the founders of the world's greatest religion all mentally disturbed?

As we look at the alternative 'explanations' of the resurrection appearances of Jesus, we are drawn to the inevitable conclusion that some people will believe anything rather than believe that a man could rise from the dead. But this was no ordinary man! His life was unique. His teaching was unique. His miracles were unique. There was never a man like this man! Did he not say that he would rise from the dead? If he really was who he claimed to be, would we not expect him to conquer death itself? To those of us who accept him as our Saviour, our Lord and our God, there is no difficulty whatever in believing in the resurrection of our Lord Jesus Christ. Those who refuse to accept his resurrection are those who refuse to accept his Lordship!

For Christians, however, there is evidence not only from the scriptures, but also from our own experience. We experience the power of Christ's name in prayer, the confirmation of

Christ's word in evangelism, and the effects of Christ's gospel in life-transforming power. In the words of an old hymn:

You ask me how I know he lives? He lives within my heart.

QUESTIONS

1. To whom did Jesus appear on the first day, as recorded in the following scriptures?

    Mark 16:9-11, John 20:11-18

    Matthew 28:8-10

    Luke 24:34, 1 Corinthians 15:5

    Luke 24:13-35

2. Who was absent on the first occasion when Jesus appeared to his disciples? See John 20:24.

3. READ John 20:26-29.

    To whom did Jesus appear a week later?

    Who was present on this occasion?

4. To whom did Jesus appear on the following other occasions?

    John 21:1-23

    Matthew 28:16-18, 1 Corinthians 15:6

    1 Corinthians 15:7

    Mark 16:14-19, Luke 24:50-52.

CHAPTER SIX

His Triumphant Ascension

The triumphant ascension of our Lord and Saviour Jesus Christ is a sadly neglected subject. Every year at Christmas, Good Friday and Easter Sunday we remember his birth, death and resurrection, but little attention is paid to 'Ascension Day', the sixth Thursday after Easter. And yet the ascension of our Lord is of great importance to us as Christians. In fact, Carl Brumback

has claimed that, if the Lord Jesus Christ had not ascended,

> **The** *infallible proof of the incarnation would be lost*
> *His sacrificial death on Calvary would have been in vain*
> *Access into the presence of God would be denied to all*
> *It would be impossible to be saved*
> *None would be indwelt or infilled by the Holy Spirit*
> *We would have no advocate* **with** *the Father*
> *The Church would be bereft of its blessed hope.*

When the disciples stood on the hill called Olivet, just three-quarters of a mile from the city of Jerusalem, they listened with eager interest as Jesus told them about the power of the Holy Spirit which was shortly to come upon them. And while they were still looking at him, *He was taken up before their very eyes and a cloud hid him from their sight* (Acts 1:9-11).

So ended the earthly life of the Lord Jesus. He had returned to his Father. His disciples were to see him no more. He had ascended into heaven. Few Christians have realised the tremendous significance of this momentous event, yet as Brumback points out, without the ascension, Christianity is meaningless. To help our understanding of the importance of this great subject, we will consider briefly eight aspects of the ascension:

Jesus demonstrated his deity

In John 6:41-42 Jesus claimed quite clearly that he had come from heaven. The Jews understandably found such a claim extremely difficult to believe. Jesus replied that the evidence that he had come *from* heaven was that he would one day be seen to return *to* heaven (v.62). The ascension is the final proof of the incarnation. If there had been any remaining doubt in the disciples' minds as to who he was, it was dispelled by the ascension. They had seen him go! Far above all principality and power and might and dominion! By his ascension Jesus demonstrated his deity.

He reclaimed his rights

When Jesus had left his Father's throne in heaven, the Bible tells us that he had emptied himself. He was essentially one with God and possessed all the attributes that make God God, but he voluntarily stripped himself of all his privileges and rightful dignity and assumed the place of a slave and was born as a human being (Philippians 2:6-7). He did this that he might come and die for us sinners. But having died for us, and having risen again the third day to demonstrate his power over death, he finally ascended forty days later. He returned to his Father and reclaimed his rights.

He had, of course, never ceased to be God. Even during the thirty three years of his life on earth as a man, he was still, always, God. But he did not choose to draw upon the attributes of deity which as God he still possessed. His miracles were performed by faith through the power of the Holy Spirit. He was completely man, yet completely God. The nature of his person will remain a mystery. Our human minds fail to grasp it. Yet this we know. He who was and is the creator and sustainer of all things, upholding all things by his powerful word, the eternal Lord of the universe, he in whom dwells all the fulness of the Godhead bodily, in whom all things consist, took upon himself the form of a servant and was made in the likeness of men. He humbled himself and became obedient to the death of the cross. And for this reason, *God has highly exalted him*. He has ascended into heaven. He has reclaimed his rights. God has put all things under his feet. He is head over all things for the Church. He is *King of Kings and Lord of Lords* and he shall reign for ever and ever. Hallelujah! By his ascension, Jesus reclaimed his rights.

He assures us of access into heaven

Without the ascension, Christ's sacrificial death on Calvary would have been in vain. In the Old Testament

'The supreme moment in the ministry of the High Priest was not at the altar but at the mercy-seat. On the Day of Atonement the High Priest became the representative of all the priests who had ministered at the altar throughout the year; the offering on that day was the one from which all other sin-offerings derived their efficacy; hence the ministry at the altar was an exceedingly solemn and sacred moment for the High Priest. But the high point of the great day came when he bore the blood of the sacrifice *beyond the veil...*

Until the blood was sprinkled on the mercy-seat, there was no atonement, no remission of sins. For no matter how perfect the sacrifice, the blood was not efficacious unless the High Priest took that blood within the veil'

But, thank God, Jesus *has* ascended. By his own blood he has entered the Holy Place as our great High Priest (Hebrews 9:12) and because he has so entered, we too may have boldness to enter (Hebrews 10:19-22). By his ascension Jesus assured us of access to heaven.

He has poured out his Spirit

But our Lord's ascension to the right hand of the majesty on high is not only the basis on which we too may enter into the presence of God himself. It was the necessary prelude to Pentecost. The descent of the Spirit was dependent on the ascent of the Son. Jesus had said:

Unless I go away the Counsellor will not come to you, but if I go I will send him to you (John 16:7).

During the time of Jesus' earthly ministry the Holy Spirit had not yet been given, for Jesus had not yet been glorified (John 7:39). But as a result of his ascension Jesus *was* glorified. Peter, preaching to the crowd on the Day of Pentecost, declared:

Exalted to the right hand of God, he has received from the Father the promised Holy Spirit and has poured out what you now see and hear (Acts 2:33).

Because of his ascension Jesus has poured out his Spirit.

We have now considered four aspects of the ascension. These all relate to the past. They tell us what Christ *has* accomplished by his ascension. The remaining four aspects relate to the present and the future. Christ's ascension is not merely a fact of history. It is vitally relevant to us here and now.

He acts as our advocate

We will discuss this subject more fully in the next chapter, but it is important to remember that it was because of the ascension that *We have someone who speaks to the Father in our defence* (1 John 2:1). As our heavenly lawyer, Jesus defends us against the accusations of Satan, 'the accuser of the brethren'.

He sends out his servants

Ephesians 4:8-11 tells us that when Jesus ascended *he led captives in his train and gave gifts to men.* It is the ascended Christ who gives men and women to the Church who will equip others for works of service – apostles, prophets, evangelists, pastors and teachers. As we work for him on earth we do it in the knowledge that he is at the right hand of God exalted in majesty and power! For more on this subject, see Chapter 17.

He prepares a place for his people

Another amazing aspect of the Lord's ascension is that he has gone to prepare a place for us. The exact details we do not know. We still see through a glass darkly (1 Corinthians 13:12). It is enough for the time being to know that we shall be where he is (John 14:3).

He awaits his advent

If I go, said Jesus, *I will come again.* He has gone, and he *is* coming. This was confirmed by the angels at his ascension:

Why do you stand here looking into the sky? This same Jesus, who has been taken from you into heaven, will come back in the same way you have seen him go into heaven (Acts 1:10-11).

But that too is a subject for another chapter (see Chapter 8).

QUESTIONS

1. READ Acts 1:7-11.
    What was Jesus talking about to the disciples?
    What happened while they were watching him?
    Which words tell us that Jesus will not stay where he is forever?
2. READ John 6:41-42, 62.
    Where did Jesus say that he had come from?
    What did he say would be the proof of this?
3. READ Philippians 2:6-11
    What did Jesus make himself? (v.7)
    What nature did he take?
    In what likeness was he made?
    What was the result of Jesus' humbling himself?
4. READ Hebrews 9:11-12
    After he had ascended, what great office did Jesus take up?
    When he ascended, where did he go?
    What did he take with him?
5. READ Hebrews 10:19-22
    Apart from Jesus, who may enter the Holy Place?
    Would this have been possible under the Old Covenant?
6. READ John 7:39 and Acts 2:33.
    Who had not yet been given?
    Why not?
    What has Jesus now done because of his ascension?
7. READ Ephesians 4:8-11
    Who ascended?
    What did he do?
    What did he give, and to whom?
8. READ John 14:2-3
    What has Jesus gone to do?
    Where is this?

CHAPTER SEVEN

His Abiding Intercession

The heavenly ministry of our Lord and Saviour Jesus Christ is closely connected with the subject of his ascension into heaven which we considered in our last chapter. It would be a mistake to imagine that when Jesus cried *It is finished* on the cross he had done all that he ever could do for his people. Certainly his work as a substitute and a sacrifice for our sins was complete. But his resurrection, ascension and glorification were in a very real sense *for us* and form an important part of our salvation. Romans 5:10 tells us that we are not only saved by his death on Calvary, but that he continues to save us by the power of his life. The Bible indicates three main ways in which he does so.

Christ is our mediator

By his death upon the cross the Lord Jesus Christ atoned for our sins. He bore on our behalf the punishment that our sins deserved. He paid the price of our redemption. By his death we are reconciled to God. Jesus died as our saviour, our substitute, our sin-bearer. Now he lives as our mediator.

When two countries have been at war and cannot come to peace on agreeable terms, a representative from a third country, not involved in the fighting, will sometimes act as a 'go-between' or mediator between the two sides. We were God's enemies because of our sin, but Jesus has not only died to save us from sin's consequences, but lives to keep us in right relationship with God. 1 Timothy 2:5 tells us that there is one God, and one mediator between God and mankind, the man Christ Jesus. It is through Jesus and Jesus alone that we have access to the Father, for it is he alone who has died to save us and it is he alone who lives to keep us.

Christ is our intercessor

But Jesus does not only live to act as our mediator at God's right hand. He is also there as our intercessor. He is able to save completely those who come to God through him because *he always lives to intercede for them* (Hebrews 7:25). While he was here on earth he *offered up prayers and petitions with loud cries and tears* (Hebrews 5:7). Now he is in heaven Jesus is constantly praying for us! He has entered *into heaven itself, now to appear for us in God's presence* (Hebrews 9:24). Why is Jesus in the presence of God? *For us!* Why is he at God's right hand? *To intercede for us!* Of course he is there by virtue of his own sovereign right. He is at God's right hand because he is King of Kings and Lord of Lords! He is there because he rules the universe and because the kingdoms of this world shall become the kingdoms of our God and of his Christ and he shall reign for ever and ever! But he is also there *for us!*

> *He ever lives above*
> *For me to intercede*
> *His all-redeeming love*
> *His precious blood to plead*
> *His blood atoned for all our race*
> *And sprinkles now the throne of grace.*

> *The Father hears him pray*
> *His dear Anointed One*
> *He cannot turn away the presence of His Son*
> *With confidence I now draw nigh*
> *And 'Father, Abba, Father' cry.*

Christ is our advocate

As our mediator Jesus has brought about our reconciliation to God. As our intercessor he is constantly praying for us. As our advocate he defends us against the false accusations of Satan.

Peter tells us that our enemy the devil prowls around like a roaring lion looking for someone to devour (1 Peter 5:8). Revelation 12:10 suggests that his role is that of an accuser. It seems as though he is allowed to appear in the court of heaven as a kind of counsel for the prosecution.

With a little sanctified imagination let us picture the scene. The heavenly judge, the judge of all the earth, is seated upon his throne. The prisoner on trial is charged with transgressing the eternal law, the word of God. We tremble as we remember that like the prisoner, we too have sinned and come short of the glory of God. It is appointed unto us once to die and after death, the judgment.

The prosecution begins his case. It is extremely lengthy, but clear and convincing. The prisoner's whole life seems under review. Sin after sin is listed – catalogues of transgressions! Surely the verdict must be guilty. At last the Prosecution brings his case to a conclusion. He insists that he has established the guilt of the prisoner. He reminds the judge of the eternal law: *The soul that sins shall surely die.* The prisoner trembles. The Prosecution demands the sentence of eternal death.

In desperation the prisoner turns to his advocate, the counsel for the defence. Our heavenly lawyer takes his stand before the judge. He acknowledges the prisoner's guilt. He does not seek to contest the charge brought against him. It is true that the prisoner is guilty. He deserves to die. Satan the accuser rubs his hands in glee – another victim!

But what is the defence saying? It is true that the prisoner is guilty, but his advocate demands his release! The punishment for the crimes of which he is guilty has already been taken. It has been borne by another. The advocate approaches the judge and kneels before him. He stretches out his arms and shows him his hands. The nail-prints are still visible. The price has been paid. The prisoner is free.

In horror Satan recoils from the sight. The nail-prints are the symbols of his greatest defeat. The accuser has been overcome once again by the blood of the Lamb (Revelation 12:10-11). He quits the courts of heaven and returns to his appointed place.

The court is silent as the advocate speaks to the prisoner: *Where is your accuser? Has no one condemned you? Then neither do I condemn you.* The prisoner is pardoned. He was demonstrably guilty and deserving of death, but he called upon the only advocate who could save him. No other defence is adequate against the accusations of the adversary. But, thank God, no other defence is necessary. We have an advocate with the Father (1 John 2:1). His name is Jesus.

QUESTIONS

1. READ Romans 5:10

   By what did Jesus save us?

   By what does he continue to save us?

2. READ 1 Timothy 2:5

   How many gods are there?

   How many mediators are there?

   Who is the mediator?

   What does this imply for those who teach that all religions lead to God and that there are many who can show the way?

3. READ Hebrews 7:25

   Who is Jesus able to save?

   Why can he save them?

4. READ 1 Peter 5:8

   Who is our adversary on earth?

   What is he trying to do?

5. READ Job 1:6, Revelation 12:10

   Who came among the sons of God before the Lord?

   What is our adversary doing in heaven?

6. READ Revelation 12:10-11, 1 John 2:1

   What is it that overcomes the accuser?

   Who is our advocate with the Father?

CHAPTER EIGHT

His Second Coming

So far we have considered the importance of doctrine, the authority of the Bible, the nature of the Godhead, the earthly life and ministry of the Lord Jesus Christ, his death, resurrection and ascension into heaven, and the nature and purpose of his heavenly ministry. We must now turn our attention to an event which has yet to take place in world history – the second coming of our Lord and Saviour Jesus Christ.

The fact of his coming

The Christian's certainty about the second coming of Christ is based upon the definite statements of the infallible word of God. The apostles and leaders of the early church taught very clearly that Christ would return. James tells us that *the Lord's coming is near* (James 5:8). Peter assures his readers that *the day of the Lord will come* (2 Peter 3:10). Jude declares *The Lord is coming* (Jude 14). It is Paul, however, who gives us the details:

For the Lord himself will come down from heaven with a loud command, with the voice of the archangel and with the trumpet-call of God…(1 Thessalonians 4:16).

In the light of this glorious prospect, John, exiled on Patmos, cried *Amen, come Lord Jesus* (Revelation 22:20).

The apostles' certainty that Christ would return was undoubtedly based on three main facts. First, they were directed by the inspiration of the Holy Spirit as they wrote the scriptures. Secondly, they remembered the promise of the angels at the ascension:

This same Jesus who has been taken from you into heaven will come in the same way as you have seen him go into heaven (Acts 1:11).

They were sure he would come because they had seen him go. And thirdly, they were sure that Jesus was coming again because they had his personal promise that they would do so:

I am going to prepare a place for you, and if I go and prepare a place for you, **I will come back** *and take you to be with me* (John 14:2-3).

On other occasions he had given them further details as to the nature and purpose of his return, telling them that *The Son of Man is going to come in his Father's glory with his holy angels* (Matthew 16:27, Mark 8:38, Luke 9:26). Christians may be quite sure that Jesus is coming. It is promised by the apostles, by the angels, and by Jesus himself.

The nature of his coming

There have been considerable differences of opinion among Bible-believing Christians as to the precise nature of the second coming of Christ. It is not possible within the scope of this book to enter into discussion upon the various points of view held by equally sincere evangelical Christians. It should be fairly safe to say, however, that there are certain facts about the return of our Lord which must be accepted if we are to be consistent in our belief in the authority of scripture.

The statement of the angels at the ascension (Acts 1:11) is sufficient evidence alone that the return of Christ will be personal, physical, and visible.

Jesus will return *personally* for it will be 'this same Jesus'. It will be 'the Lord himself' who will descend from heaven (1 Thessalonians 4:16).

Jesus will return *physically,* for he is coming 'in the same way' as they saw him go. He will descend with the same resurrection body with which they saw him ascend.

And Jesus will return *visibly,* for he will return 'in the same way as *you have seen him go*'. The early disciples were privileged to see him go into heaven. How marvellous to consider that we may very well be among those who are privileged to see him return!

The purpose of his coming

Since the second coming has yet to take place, all that we know about it is what God has chosen to reveal in his word. As we examine the New Testament there seem to be five main purposes of our Lord's return.

First, he is coming for his church. 1 Thessalonians 4:16-17 tells us that when the Lord returns the dead in Christ will rise first. After that we who are still alive and are left will be caught up with them in the clouds to meet the Lord in the air; and so we will be with the Lord for ever.

Jesus is coming in order that we might meet him and be with him for ever. Hallelujah!

Secondly, Jesus is coming for the destruction of death. In those majestic verses in 1 Corinthians 15:51-57 Paul gives us another description of the events which will take place when the trumpet sounds. *Then,* he says, *the saying that is written will come true: Death has been swallowed up in victory* (v.54).

Thirdly, Jesus is coming to judge the world. Those who have rejected him will be judged, for the Lord Jesus will be revealed from heaven with his powerful angels in blazing fire. He will punish those who do not know God and do not obey the gospel of our Lord Jesus Christ. They will be punished with everlasting destruction, shut out from the presence of the Lord and the majesty of his power (2 Thessalonians 1:7-9).

True Christians, of course, will not be judged for their sins. Our sins were judged at Calvary. It does seem, however, that there is to be a judgment for Christians which is related to reward for service (1 Corinthians 3:11-15).

Closely connected with the fact that Jesus is coming as judge is the glorious truth that he is coming as king. He is coming to reign (Revelation 20:4, 6). Paul tells us that Jesus must reign until he has put all his enemies under his feet (1 Corinthians 15:25). The kingdoms of this world are to become the kingdom of our God and of his Christ and *He shall reign for ever and ever* (Revelation 11:15).

Finally, Jesus is coming to make all things new. There will be no more death, no more sorrow, or crying, or any more pain; they will all have passed away (Revelation 21:4-5). There are to be new heavens and a new earth in which righteousness will dwell (2 Peter 3:13).   What a wonderful promise! What a blessed hope! Thank God, Jesus is coming!

Preparation for his coming

In the light of this divine revelation, the Bible tells us that we must be prepared. It is not for us to know the times or the seasons which the Father has put under his own authority (Acts 1:7). Jesus says that no one knows the day or hour when he will come again (Mark 13:32). The day of the Lord will be as unexpected as a thief in the night (1 Thessalonians 5:2). We do not need to know the time of his coming. But we *do* need to be ready.

In Matthew 24:42-51 Jesus warns us of the dangers of those who say, 'My master is staying away a long time'. In the next chapter he tells us that we are to be ready by keeping watch (v. 13). We are to be ready by making sure that we are using faithfully the talents which the Lord has entrusted to our care (Matthew 25:14-30). If we do, we may be sure that we too will hear the commendation of our Lord when he comes:

Well done, good and faithful servant... come and share your master's happiness.

In the light of the unthinkable alternative (v.30), may God help us to be ready.

QUESTIONS

1. READ James 5:8, 2 Peter 3:10, 1 Thessalonians 4:16

   Which words tell us about the return of our Lord?

   What position in the church did the men who made these statements hold?

2. READ 2 Peter 1:21, Acts 1:11, John 14:2-3.

   Who inspired the apostles to write the scriptures?

   What promise did the angels give them?

   What promise had Jesus already given them?

3. READ Matthew 16:27, Mark 8:38, Luke 9:26.

   What further details does Jesus add to his promise in these verses?

4. READ Acts 1:11. What words in this statement show that the Lord's return will be:

   physical

   personal

   visible?

5. READ 1 Thessalonians 4:16-17.

   Who rises first?

   Who next?

   What for?

   Will we ever be separated from the Lord?

6. READ 1 Corinthians 15:51-57. List as many as you can of the events that will happen 'when the trumpet sounds'.

7. READ 2 Thessalonians 1:7-9

   Who is to be judged?

   What for?

   What will be the punishment?

8. READ 1 Corinthians 3:11-15

   Will there be a judgment for Christians?

   If so, what will it be for?

9. READ Revelation 21:4-5, 2 Peter 3:13

   What will end when Jesus comes?

   What will be new?

   What will they be like?

10. How are we to be ready for the Lord's coming according to:

    Matthew 24:42-51

    Matthew 25:1-13

    Matthew 25:14-30?

CHAPTER NINE

The Fall of Man

So far we have devoted most of our attention to the person and ministry of our Lord Jesus Christ. It is now time to direct our thoughts to the subject of the Fall of Man. The Bible teaches that when God made man he made him perfect and put him in a perfect creation. In Genesis 1:27 we read that God created man and woman in his own image and *God saw **all** that he had made, and it was very good* (v.31). In the next chapter we are told that

The Lord commanded the man, 'You are free to eat from any tree in the garden, but you must not eat from the tree of the knowledge of good and evil, for when you eat from it you will surely die (Genesis 2:16-17).

Sadly, however, we read in Chapter 3 how Adam and Eve were tempted by Satan and disobeyed God by eating this fruit. This first act of disobedience on the part of mankind is known as *The Fall of Man* ('Man' here meaning both man and woman of course – mankind). As we shall see as we examine the subject more closely, however, *the Fall* is not just something in which Adam and Eve had a part, but was an act of rebellion against God in which we ourselves are all personally involved.

The nature of the Fall

The seriousness of Adam's sin lies not merely in the fact that he ate the forbidden fruit, but in the reasons why he did so. Through the influence of Satan he came first to *doubt* God's word (Genesis 3:1) and then positively to *disbelieve* it (3:4). This resulted in his final *disobedience* (3:6). How clearly his sin typifies those of countless generations of human beings ever since! We refuse to take God's statement seriously, we prefer not to believe what he has said, and our disbelief, like Adam and Eve's, results in disobedience - and death.

The seriousness of the Fall

The seriousness of sin – both Adam's and ours – is seen when we consider the nature of the commands we have broken. God's command to Adam and Eve, like all the laws he has given to the human race, resulted from God's authority, his goodness, his wisdom and justice, his faithfulness, grace and love. In disobeying, we reject his authority, doubt his goodness, dispute his wisdom and justice, deny his faithfulness, spurn his grace and refuse his love. Adam's sin was the contradiction of all God's perfection. The consequences are hardly surprising.

The consequences of the Fall

The first effects of the Fall are seen in man's attitude to God. Adam and Eve experienced a sense of fear and shame they had never known before. They knew that they were naked (3:7) and were afraid (3:10). Instead of enjoying the presence of God they hid themselves from the Lord (3:8).

So the separation from God which sin causes results partly from our sense of shame. But it is also the inevitable requirement of God's holiness. His eyes are too pure to look at evil. He cannot be complacent towards sin. Adam and Eve were driven out of the Garden of Eden (3:24) and by their disobedience the entire human race was separated from God.

As time went by, man's sinful condition grew worse and worse. Cain slew Abel (Genesis 4:8). Lamech committed polygamy (4:19) and murder (4:23). Mankind's wickedness became very great (6:5). The Fall has had a lasting effect. Even the physical creation was affected. God cursed the ground because of Adam's sin (3:17) and even now the whole creation is groaning in pain (Romans 8:22). And not only pain, but death. God had warned, *When you eat of it you will surely die* (Genesis 2:17). In disbelief and disobedience mankind has chosen to ignore God's warning. The consequences were inescapable. The sentence of divine justice must be pronounced: *Dust you are, and to dust you will return* (Genesis 3:19).

The imputation of the Fall

As we have seen, Adam's sin was to affect not only himself and his immediate family, but the entire human race as well. As the father of our race he represents us all. There is a sense in which when he sinned, we all sinned. By his sin, he brought sin and death to us all. This is something which is made clear in Romans 5:12-14:

When Adam sinned, sin entered the entire human race. His sin spread death throughout all the world, so everything began to grow old and die, for all sinned. We know that it was Adam's sin that caused this, because although, of course, people were sinning from the time of Adam until Moses, God did not in those days judge them guilty of death for breaking his laws – because he had not yet given his laws to them, nor told them what he wanted them to do. So when their bodies died it was not for their own sins, since they themselves had never disobeyed God's special law against eating the forbidden fruit, as Adam had (Living Bible).

What we are told here is that Adam's sin infected the entire human race. This is proved by the fact that all the people who lived between Adam and Moses had received no specific commandment from God. (Adam had received a specific command from God with regard to the fruit, and Moses had received the Law and the Ten Commandments, but no specific commandments were given to those who lived in between). Yet all these people died. They could not have died for breaking God's specific commandments, for they had not been given any. Therefore, Paul reasons, they died as a result of Adam's sin. His sin is imputed to us all.

There have been those who have argued that this is unfair. Why should I die as a result of something Adam did? Yet the Bible makes it clear that this is perfectly fair, for I have sinned too. By my actions I have ratified (agreed with) Adam's rebellion, for I too have rebelled against God. The sad fact is that, if I had been in Adam's place, I would have done exactly the same as he did. As a result of Adam's sin death has come to all mankind, but this is perfectly fair, *for all have sinned.* The Fall is something in which we are all personally involved.

Salvation from the Fall

How grateful we must be, then, that when God passed judgment upon the human race because of Adam's sin, he had already prepared a way by which man might be restored. Satan had won a great victory over our first parents when his temptations caused their fall. But when the first Adam failed, God had prepared a second 'Adam', one of his descendants, the offspring of the woman who would crush the serpent's head (Genesis 3:15).

The first Adam, as the representative head of the human race, was defeated. The last Adam (the Lord Jesus Christ) came that he might conquer. He succeeded where Adam failed. He is the head of a new race, a redeemed humanity, the people of God, the Church. Those who are in Adam (the unsaved) still reap the effects of Adam's sin. Those who are in Christ (those who are saved) are to be rescued from the consequences of the Fall. We still live in a fallen world. Our bodies are still subject to death. But we are no longer separated from God! We have been restored to fellowship! We have eternal life! And the day is coming – a day for which the whole of creation is longing – when even our bodies will be redeemed! The effects of the curse will be lifted! God will reveal his glory in us. The sons of God will be revealed to the entire universe. Creation itself will be delivered from its bondage to decay into the glorious freedom of the children of God (Romans 8:18-23).

What a contrast between Adam and Christ! Adam by his sin caused many to be sinners. By his one offence came judgment and condemnation and death. But as by the offence of one man (Adam) judgment came upon all mankind, even so, thank God, by the righteousness of one man (Christ), the free gift of justification became available to all:

For if, by the trespass of the one man, death reigned through that one man, how much more will those who receive God's abundant provision of grace and the gift of righteousness reign in life through the one man Jesus Christ.

Consequently, just as the result of one trespass was condemnation for all men, so also the result of one act of righteousness was justification that brings life for all men. For just as through the disobedience of the one man the many were made sinners, so also through the obedience of the one man the many will be made righteous.

The law was added so that the trespass might increase. But where sin increased, grace increased all the more, so that, just as sin reigned in death, so also grace might reign through righteousness to bring eternal life through Jesus Christ our Lord (Romans 5:17-21).

QUESTIONS

1. READ Genesis 1:27

   In whose likeness was man created?

   How does God describe all that he had made?

2. READ Genesis 2:16-17

   What simple commandment is here given to Adam?

3. READ Genesis 3:1, 4, 6.

   Which words show how doubt in God's word was planted?

   Which words show how disbelief followed?

   Which words show how disobedience followed?

4. READ Genesis 3:7-8, 24

   What did Adam and Eve realise for the first time?

   How did this affect their relationship with God?

   What happened to them as a result of their sin?

5. READ Genesis 3:17, Romans 8:22

   How has creation been affected by Adam's sin?

6. READ Genesis 2:17 and 3:19.

   What was God's warning?

   What was the divine sentence?

7. READ Genesis 3:15 and 1 Corinthians 15:45, 47

   What words point forward to a 'second Adam'?

   Who is the second Adam?

8. READ Romans 8:18-23

   From what and into what will creation be delivered?

   What will the children of God have then?

CHAPTER TEN

Saved through Faith

In the last chapter we considered the nature and serious consequences of man's sin. But we saw too that, even at the time of the fall of man in the garden of Eden, God promised that the offspring of the woman would crush the serpent's head. This was a promise of the coming of Christ who was to deliver mankind from sin and its consequences. What was lost for us by Adam's sin has been regained for us by Christ's righteousness (Romans 5).

This deliverance from sin brought about by Christ though his atoning death on the cross is known as *salvation.* The Concise Oxford Dictionary defines salvation as *Deliverance from sin and its consequences and admission to heaven brought about by Christ.*

As we saw in Chapter 4, salvation is necessary because all have sinned and because the consequences of sin are so very serious. God has wonderfully made salvation possible by sending his Son Jesus to die on the cross for our sins. All that he requires of us is that we repent and believe the gospel.

The scriptures listed on the following pages help us to gain a clear understanding of the nature of our salvation. They are also a useful source of important verses to use in leading others to Christ. You may feel that you want to memorise some of them, or at least to try to remember where to find them.

The need for salvation

The Universality of Sin

1 Kings 8:46	There is no one who does not sin
Psalm 14:3	There is no one who does good, not even one
Ecclesiastes 7:20	There is not a righteous man on the earth who does what is right and never sins

Romans 3:23	All have sinned…
Galatians 3:22	The whole world is a prisoner to sin
1 John 1:8	If we claim to be without sin we deceive ourselves
1 John 5:19	The whole world is under the control of the evil one

The Consequences of Sin

Now, in this life, the sinner: is sick (Matthew 9:12, Mark 2:17)

cannot understand spiritual things (1 Corinthians 2:14)

has a blinded mind (2 Corinthians 4:4)

has a defiled conscience (Titus 1:15)

is a fool (Romans 1:22)

is an enemy of the cross of Christ (Philippians 3:18)

loves darkness (John 3:19)

is without Christ, hope, or God (Ephesians 2:12)

cannot cease from sin (2 Peter 2:14)

is on the way to destruction (Matthew 7:18-19)

has a lost soul (Matthew 16:26, 18:11)

is worthy of death (Romans 1:32)

is dead in sins (Colossians 2:13)

After death, the sinner faces judgment and punishment:

John 3:36	…whoever rejects the Son will not see life, for God's wrath remains on him
Acts 17:31	…he has set a day when he will judge the world with justice by the man he has appointed
Colossians 3:6	…the wrath of God is coming…

2 Thessalonians 1:7-9   The Lord Jesus will be revealed from heaven with his powerful angels in blazing fire. He will punish those who do not know God and do not obey the gospel of our Lord Jesus Christ. They will be punished with everlasting destruction and shut out from the presence of the Lord and the majesty of his power

Hebrews 9:27   Man is destined to die once, and after that to face judgment

Jesus described this punishment as:

hell fire (Matthew 5:22)

outer darkness (Matthew 8:12)

everlasting punishment (Matthew 25:46)

and said that whoever does not believe stands condemned already (John 3:18).

The means of salvation

God's remedy – the death of his Son

Romans 5:6, 8, 10...*just at the right time, when we were still powerless, Christ died for the ungodly... God demonstrates his own love for us in this: while we were still sinners, Christ dies for us...When we were God's enemies we were reconciled to him through the death of his Son.*

1 Timothy 1:15   Christ Jesus came into the world to save sinners

1 Peter 3:18   Christ died for sins once for all, the righteous for the unrighteous, to bring you to God

Man's responsibility – repentance and faith

Luke 13:3	...unless you **repent**, you... will perish
Luke 24:47 nations	**Repentance** ...will be preached... to all
Acts 2:38	**Repent**, and be baptised every one...
Acts 3:19	**Repent**, then, and turn to God
Acts 17:30	...but now he commands all people everywhere to **repent**
John 3:16	For God so loved the world that he gave his one and only Son, that whoever believes in him shall not perish but have eternal life.
Acts 10:43	everyone who **believes** in him receives forgiveness of sins
Romans 1:16	the gospel is the power of God for the Salvation of everyone who believes
Romans 5:1	... we have been justified by faith
Galatians 2:16	...know that a man is not justified by observing the law, but by faith in Jesus Christ
Ephesians 2:8	By grace you have been saved, through faith

Are you sure that when you die you will go to heaven? If not, turn from your sin right now and trust Jesus to save you.

QUESTIONS

1. READ Romans 3:23, 1 John 1:8
   What do these verses teach us?

2. READ Ephesians 2:12
   What is the condition of those who are without Christ?

3. READ Mark 16:16
   Who will be condemned?

4. READ Romans 5:6, 8, 10
   How does God show his love to us?

5. READ 1 Timothy 1:15
   Why did Jesus come into the world?

6. READ Ephesians 2:8
   How are we saved?

7. READ John 3:16
   What is promised to those who believe?

CHAPTER ELEVEN

The Blood of Christ

We have already considered the substitutionary atoning death of Christ in an earlier chapter. He died in our place so that our sins could be forgiven. In doing so, of course, he *shed his blood* for us. This is important because we are told in Hebrews 9:22 that *without the shedding of blood there is no forgiveness* and in Leviticus 17:11 that *it is the blood that makes atonement.*

Perhaps the best example of the importance of the blood in the Old Testament is the story of the Passover. God had decreed that all the firstborn of the land of Egypt were to die. The Israelites were to sacrifice a lamb and mark the doorposts and lintel of their houses with its blood. In Exodus 12:13 God said, *When I see the blood, I will **pass over** you.* Only those who were marked with the blood of the lamb could escape death. This was an amazing prophetic picture of how today only those who have put their trust in the atoning blood of Christ, the lamb of God who takes away the sins of the world (John 1:29), will escape the death penalty which is the result of sin. Thank God, *Christ our Passover has been sacrificed for us* (1 Corinthians 5:7).

In fact the New Testament makes it clear that the sacrifices of the Old Testament were only a picture of what was to come. They could not *take away* sin (Hebrews 10:4). They were part of the old covenant, whereas Jesus is the mediator of a new and better covenant which is ratified in his blood (Matthew 26:28, Mark 14:24, Luke 22:20). These verses make it clear that the purpose of the shedding of Christ's blood was the *remission of our sins.* But there are many other benefits which we derive from having our sins forgiven through faith in Christ's blood:

Cleansing

Sin defiles, but thank God, by faith in Christ's shed blood we can be made clean. *The blood of Jesus his Son purifies us from every sin* (1 John 1:7). Jesus loves us and has *freed us from our sins by his own blood* (Revelation 1:5). Our robes are made white in the blood of the Lamb (Revelation 7:14).

Redemption

Furthermore, in Jesus we have *redemption through his blood* (Ephesians 1:7, Colossians 1:14). Redemption means *deliverance from evil by the payment of a price.* Prisoners of war could be released on the payment of a ransom. We were once the captives of sin, but Jesus has paid the price of our release. He has *redeemed* us. And the price he paid was the shedding of his blood. Corruptible things – even silver or gold – could never have paid the price for us. Only the blood of Christ was sufficiently precious (1 Peter 1:18-19). And because of the value of that blood, the redemption he has obtained for us is eternal (Hebrews 9:12). Throughout the eternal ages there will be those from every tribe and language and people and nation who will surround his throne in worship and adoration, crying, *You were slain, and with your blood you purchased men for God* (Revelation 5:9).

Propitiation

Another great benefit that results from the shedding of Christ's blood is that by it God's holy anger has been appeased. This is known as *propitiation* which means *the removal of wrath by the offering of a gift.* Romans 3:25 teaches us that Jesus is an atoning sacrifice to turn aside God's anger and take away our sins. This is *through faith in his blood* which was shed for our sins, *and not for ours only but **for the sins of the whole world*** (1 John 2:2). God was justly angry at the sins of the world, but his anger has been appeased by the offering of the blood of his Son.

Reconciliation

And resulting from propitiation is reconciliation. Once we were enemies of God, but *when we were enemies we were reconciled to God through the death of his Son* (Romans 5:10). He made peace *through his blood shed on the cross* (Colossians 1:20) because, by Jesus, God wanted to reconcile all things to himself. Thank God, we are no longer enemies, but sons, redeemed that we might receive adoption as sons and even as heirs (Galatians 4:4-7).

Justification

One of the reasons that God has been able to adopt us into his family is that we have been justified. This means that he has declared us righteous. He will not have sinners in his family, but by Christ's blood we have been cleansed. God counts us as righteous. He looks on us as though we had never sinned at all! Amazing grace! Being justified by faith we have peace with God (reconciliation) through our Lord Jesus Christ (Romans 5:1). And because we are justified by his blood we shall also be saved from wrath though him (Romans 5:9).

Sanctification

Yet another aspect of our salvation which relates to the blood of Christ is our sanctification. This refers to our actually becoming righteous (holy) in practical everyday terms. But this is such an important subject that we shall devote an entire chapter to it later.

Access

As sinners, God would not allow us to enter his holy presence. But now, through Christ's blood, we have been cleansed, reconciled, justified, sanctified! Now he bids us enter. We have been brought near by the blood of Christ (Ephesians 2:13).

Therefore, brothers, since we have confidence to enter the most holy place by the blood of Jesus... let us draw near (Hebrews 10:19).

The veil of the temple has been split from the top to the bottom. Sinful man may enter the presence of a holy God, for Christ has shed his blood and died. It cost Jesus so much for us to be able to enter God's presence. Ought we not to draw near to him more often?

Victory over the devil's false accusations

Finally, we notice that we may overcome the devil's false accusations by the blood of the lamb (Revelation 12:10-11). It should be noticed at this stage, however, that some Christians have taken this thought too far. There is in the Bible no justification whatever for 'pleading the blood' against demons, or asking God to 'cover with the blood' the building, the car, or our loved ones for their protection (as we sometimes hear some Christians pray). Jesus told his disciples to cast out demons *in his name* (not with his blood), and it is important to realise that the blood of the Passover lamb was sprinkled on the doorposts to avert *God's* judgment, not an attack of the devil.

In fact, the Bible teaches very clearly that the blood speaks to *God*. Revelation 12:11 needs to be read in its context, and as we do so we see that the blood of the lamb is used to overcome the daily accusations of the devil (v.10). Satan will constantly seek to remind us that we are sinners. But by the blood of the lamb we have been cleansed, redeemed and justified. By that blood we are in right standing with God. We need not surrender to the constant accusations of the enemy. Jesus has shed his blood for us. We are his and his forever. And nothing that Satan can say can alter that.

QUESTIONS

1. READ Hebrews 9:22

   What is necessary for the remission of sins?

2. READ Exodus 12:13

   What does God say here?

3. READ John 1:29, 1 Corinthians 5:7

   Who is the lamb of God?

   What happened to him?

4. READ 1 John 1:7, Revelation 1:5

   What does the blood of Jesus do?

5. READ Ephesians 1:7, Colossians 1:14, 1 Peter 1:18-19

   What has happened to us because Christ has shed his blood for us?

6. READ Romans 5:10

   What were we to God?

   What does the death of his Son do for us?

7. READ Colossians 1:20, Galatians 4:4-7

   What did Jesus make through his blood shed on the cross?

   For what purpose?

   What is the result of reconciliation?

8. READ Romans 5:1

   As well as peace with God (reconciliation) what else has happened because of Jesus?

9. READ Ephesians 2:13, Hebrews 10:19

   From whom were we far away?

   Into where may we draw near by the blood of Christ?

10. READ Revelation 12:10-11

    By what are the accusations of the devil overcome?

CHAPTER TWELVE

The New Birth

One of the most exciting facts about the wonderful salvation that God has so graciously provided for us is that although it is simple enough for a child to receive it, it is nevertheless so infinitely complex that our minds fail to grasp its full significance. In fact, so great is the theme of salvation that the Bible must approach it from many angles, presenting its many different aspects to us in a great variety of ways. In the last two chapters, for example, we saw that we are saved by faith in the shed blood of the Lord Jesus Christ, and we were able to list no fewer than eight different benefits which are ours simply because Jesus died for us.

We must now turn our attention to another closely connected subject – the new birth, or 'regeneration'. When we receive Jesus as our Saviour, we are not only *saved* from our sins and their consequences, but we actually become a *new creation* in Christ (2 Corinthians 5:17) and this comes about by our being *born again.*

New life needed

In John 3 Jesus made it abundantly plain that if we are to enter heaven, we must be born again (verses 3, 5, 7). Nicodemus was not only a deeply religious man, but he would have been well educated by the standards of his day and a man of considerable social and political position. He even acknowledged that Jesus was a teacher who had come from God. He recognised that the miracles that Jesus was performing were undoubtedly an indication that God was with him (v.2). Yet it was to this man that Jesus solemnly declared, *You must be born again* (v.7). In fact, if *anyone* is to see the kingdom of God, they must be born again (v.3).

Jesus is here teaching very clearly that our education, our social or political position, even our religion, will not save us. Whatever we do, we are so far short of God's standards and glory that our only hope is to become an entirely new person altogether! We must be born again! We must become a *new creation.* Ephesians 2 tells us that before we were saved we were *dead* in sins (v.1), but that by God's grace he has *made us alive* (v.5), and this he did when we put our trust in Christ as Saviour (v.8). We are no longer *objects of wrath* (v.3), but have been born again into God's family and are now children of God.

New life provided

As we have seen in earlier chapters, it is God who has made full provision for our salvation by sending his Son Jesus to die on the cross for our sins. It is God who has saved us. We have done nothing towards it. It is all of his grace.

And what is true of what Jesus did at Calvary is true of our conversion. It was God who took the initiative. The new birth has its origin in the will of God. We are children *born not of natural descent, nor of human decision or a husband's will, but born of God* (John 1:13). He *chose to give us birth through the word of truth* (James 1:18). It is the will of God that men and women be born again.

The new birth is *not of natural descent* - it cannot be inherited from our parents. It is not *of human decision* – it is in no way a natural event. It is not by *a husband's will* – it cannot be humanly imparted. God and God alone can regenerate. This fact is emphasised by the frequently recurring phrase *born of God* (John 1:13, 1 John 3:9, 4:7, 5:1, 4, 18), and the expressions *born of the Spirit* (John 3:5) and *rebirth by the Holy Spirit* (Titus 3:5) show us which person of the Godhead is the agent of the new birth. We are born again by the agency of the Holy Spirit.

But what is the instrument the Spirit uses? James 1:18 tells us that he gave us rebirth *through the word of truth,* and 1 Peter 1:23 assures us that we are *born again, not of perishable seed, but of imperishable, through the living and enduring word of God.* The preaching of the word of God under the anointing of the Holy Spirit creates by God's grace an opportunity for the sinner to repent and believe the gospel. If he does so, he is instantaneously regenerated by the Holy Spirit. He is born again.

Passages such as John 3:1-16, John 1:12-13, and 1 John 5:1 make it clear that it is those who believe who are born of God, and that, therefore, the new birth is an instantaneous and complete work of the Holy Spirit upon initial faith in our Lord Jesus Christ.

New life in action

The first great result of our being born again is that we immediately become children of God (John 1:12-13). Accordingly we are made partakers of the divine nature and should show that nature in our lives. The two great aspects of God's personality which John emphasises in his first letter are love and righteousness, and he naturally expects those who are *born of God* to manifest these qualities (1 John 4:7, 1 John 2:29).

If we really are the children of God then we should live like it. And that means living in victory. The world around us will claim our attention and our loyalty. But we have been born anew. We belong to a different society. We are members of the heavenly family. *Everyone who is born of God is victorious over the world* (1 John 5:4).

Sin will always be present to tempt us. But we are *dead to sin and alive to God* (Romans 6:11) and consequently we do not habitually practise sin because God's nature is in us because we are born of God (1 John 3:9). This verse does not mean that if we sin at all we cannot possibly be born again. It refers to habitual attitudes, not to occasional actions. John was writing his letter to combat the Gnostic heresy that taught that knowledge was superior to righteousness and that right living was not important! Christians do sin, but, thank God, 1 John 1:9 tells us that

if we confess our sins, he is faithful and just, and will forgive us our sins, and purify us from all unrighteousness.

However, God has made provision for us to live in victory. He has implanted within us his own divine nature. We have been born again. We are his children. Our old sinful nature was crucified with Christ (Romans 6:6) and we need no longer listen to its desires. We are new creatures in Christ. Old things have passed away. All things have become new (2 Corinthians 5:17). That is why we not only have victory over the world and over sin; we also have victory over the devil:

We know that anyone born of God does not deliberately and knowingly practise committing sin, but the One who was begotten of God carefully watches over and protects him – Christ's divine presence within him preserves against the evil – and the wicked one does not lay hold, get a grip on him or touch him (1 John 5:18, Amplified Bible).

There is absolutely no need to live in defeat! We are born again. We are born of *GOD!* Let us live as his children. We should live in victory!

QUESTIONS

1. READ 2 Corinthians 5:17

   If a person is 'in Christ', what are they?

2. READ John 3:3, 5, 7

   What one thing is stressed as necessary to enter heaven?

3. READ Ephesians 2:1, 5

   What were we before we became Christians?

   What are we now?

4. READ John 3:5, Titus 3:5

   Which person of the Godhead is the one who brings about the new birth?

5. READ What does the Holy Spirit use to give us new life according to:

   James 1:18

   1 Peter 1:23?

6. READ John 1:12-13

   What is the first great result of our being born again?

7. READ Romans 6:11, 1 John 3:9

   What are we dead to?

   What are we alive to?

   What are the consequences?

8. READ 1 John 1:9

   What promises are given to Christians who find that they have sinned? (If you don't know this verse already, it would be good to memorise it).

CHAPTER THIRTEEN

Water Baptism

Once we have been born again, the first step of obedience that is required of us is that we should be baptised in water. In this chapter we will consider various forms of 'baptism' practised in the church today in the light of the true meaning of the word *baptise*, and will then go on to examine why, how, and when we should be baptised. Finally we will take a look at some serious misunderstandings and misuse of baptism.

Methods of baptism

Largely speaking today there are two very different kinds of baptism. First, there is 'infant baptism'. This is perhaps the most common form of 'baptism' today. It is practised by the Roman Catholics, the Church of England, Methodists and others. During the 'christening' service the minister sprinkles the child's head with water.

The other form of baptism in common use today is believers' baptism by immersion. This is practised mainly by Baptists, Pentecostals, and the 'new churches'. It is quite different from 'infant baptism' because only believers are baptised. This means that no baby is ever baptised because he or she is too young to be a believer in Jesus. Another difference is that the person being baptised is not just sprinkled, but is completely immersed – that is, dipped – under the water. These, then, are the two main kinds of baptism today. We shall now seek to answer the question, *Which kind is right?* And in order to do so we will first consider the meaning of the word 'baptise'.

The meaning of baptism

For the meaning of a word it is usual to turn to a dictionary. The Concise Oxford Dictionary defines baptism as follows:

Religious rite of immersing (person) in, or sprinkling with, water in sign of purification and admission to the Church accompanied by name-giving.

Although this is a fair statement of how the word 'baptism' is used in English today, it is not the meaning of the Greek word used in the New Testament when Jesus commanded his disciples to baptise. We will say more about this under the heading *The mode of baptism*, so for the moment we will confine ourselves to the meaning of the Greek word *baptizo* which means 'I baptise'. In the Greek language *baptizo* can mean 'submerge', 'overwhelm', or 'immerse', but never 'sprinkle'. If a Greek wanted to say 'I sprinkle', he would say *rhantizo*, and if Jesus had intended his followers to be sprinkled he would have talked about 'rhantism' not 'baptism'! In short, the Greek word *baptizo* cannot mean 'I sprinkle', and so if a person has only been sprinkled, they have not really been baptised, for to be baptised means to be immersed.

Having, then, considered the meaning of the word 'baptism', we shall now ask the question, *Why is it important for a Christian to be baptised?* What are our motives for being baptised?

Motives for baptism

1. Jesus was baptised

   In John 12:26 Jesus told us that if we serve him we must follow him. Similarly 1 Peter 2:21 tells us that we should follow in the steps of Jesus. We see from these verses that as Christians we should follow Christ's example. Since Jesus was baptised (Matthew 3:13-17), it follows that we should be.

2. To fulfil all righteousness

   When Jesus asked John the Baptist to baptise him, John protested on the grounds that he was not worthy to baptise Jesus. To this Jesus replied: *Let it be so now; it is proper for us to do this to fulfil all righteousness* (Matthew 3:15). If Jesus who was sinless felt it necessary to be baptised in order to 'fulfil all righteousness' he clearly felt that he would not have remained completely righteous if he had not been baptised. It was a good thing to do, and *Anyone who knows the good he ought to do and doesn't do it sins* (James 4:17). How much more then ought we to be baptised?

3. Jesus commanded it

This is the simplest, strongest and most obvious reason for baptism. In Matthew 28:19-20 Jesus said:

Therefore go and make disciples of all nations, baptising them in the name of the Father and of the Son and of the Holy Spirit, teaching them to obey everything I have commanded you...

To refuse to be baptised is to disobey Jesus. To delay one's decision to be baptised is to continue in disobedience.

4. Its connection with the baptism in the Holy Spirit

The following scriptures show us that, although the baptism in the Spirit is different from baptism in water, there is nevertheless a very important link between them (Matthew 3:11, Mark 1:8, Luke 3:16, John 1:33, Acts 1:5, Acts 2:38, Acts 11:16). However, we will deal with the important subject of the baptism in the Holy Spirit in Chapter Fifteen.

5. Baptism is a symbol of death, burial and resurrection

In Romans 6:2 we are told that as Christians we are 'dead to sin'. Our old sinful nature was 'crucified with Christ' (v.6). Accordingly we must count ourselves to be 'dead to sin, but alive to God' (v.11). Putting it simply, a dead body cannot sin. It cannot, for example, tell lies, kill or steal. It is incapable of sinning! So, since the Bible tells us to think of ourselves as dead as far as sin is concerned, when we are tempted we should say, *No, I am dead to sin. I am only alive for*

God. As far as sin is concerned, I'm dead. And as long as you think of yourself as dead to sin, you will be!

Now the thing about dead people is that they have to be buried. This is where baptism in water comes in. Romans 6:3-4 tells us that we are buried by baptism into Christ's death. Baptism, then, is a picture or symbol of the burial and resurrection of Christ. When we are baptised we are showing our identification and union with Christ in his death, burial, and resurrection. We, too, are dead (to sin). We must, therefore, be buried (in baptism). As we come up out of the water, we come up, so to speak, out of the grave, raised from the dead (old life) to live a new life, free from sin.

God's motive

So far we have given five scriptural reasons why we should be baptised. But the question naturally arises, 'But *why* does God command baptism? It seems such an odd thing to do!' Of course, on the face of it, baptism does seem an unusual ceremony; but then, so too is the Communion Service (see Chapter Fourteen) humanly speaking. We must tread very carefully here. It is enough that God has commanded these things. It is not our prerogative to ask why God has commanded them. However, perhaps we could reverently suggest – and it is only a suggestion – a reason why God has commanded that we should undergo this apparently strange ceremony.

It is a simple fact of human nature that we remember relatively little of what we hear. We remember rather more of what we hear *and see.* We remember even more of what we hear and see *and take part in.* Now in baptism, we do not merely hear that we are dead, but we see and take part in our own burial service! God wants us to know that we are dead to sin and alive to him. He wants us to count on it. He wants us to remember it. So he gets us to act out our identification with Christ's death, burial and resurrection.

Whenever I see another Christian baptised I remember my own baptism. I remember that I too have been buried with Christ, that I too am dead to sin and alive to God through Jesus Christ our Lord. I am reminded that I ought to be living for Jesus.

The mode of baptism

As we saw when we considered the meaning of the word 'baptism', the dictionary says that a person may be baptised by either immersion or sprinkling. But apart from the fact that the Greek word *baptizo* simply means 'immerse' and not 'sprinkle', the Bible itself makes it perfectly clear that in New Testament times baptism was always by immersion.

For one thing, as we saw from Romans 6, baptism is a picture of burial. If baptism had been by sprinkling in the days of the apostle Paul, his readers would have found the symbolism of such passages completely meaningless. We do not sprinkle people with earth when we bury them. We cover them.

It was because baptism was always by immersion in the New Testament that John baptised '*in* the River Jordan' (Matthew 3:6, Mark 1:5, 9). If he had merely sprinkled those he baptised, he would presumably have done so *on the banks* of Jordan and not *in* it. This is why he baptised at Aenon, because *there was plenty of water* (John 3:23). You don't need plenty of water to sprinkle people!

In Matthew 3:16 we are told that Jesus *went up out of the water* after his baptism, clearly implying that he had *gone down into* it. Similarly in Acts 8:38 we are told that when Philip baptised the eunuch, *both Philip and the eunuch went down into the water* and that they *came up out of the water.* Again this shows that baptism was by immersion.

Of course there are occasions in scripture when baptism is not described so fully as in the passages we have just mentioned. So those who practise sprinkling argue that for all we know such people may have been sprinkled! However, in the absence of any positive statement to this effect in the New Testament, it would be foolish to base our doctrines on so doubtful an assumption. And, of course, we do know how these people were baptised, for in being told that they were 'baptised' at all we are told that they were immersed, for that is the meaning of the word *baptizo*. Indeed, there is no doubt whatsoever that in the light of holy scripture we may confident reassert that *if a person has only been sprinkled, they have not really been baptised.*

The moment of baptism

Having now shown very clearly that the biblical mode of baptism was by immersion, we must turn our attention to the subject of the moment of baptism. In other words, *when* should a person be baptised?

The Bible is quite clear on this point too. Although no statement is made as to how old a person ought to be before they are baptised, we are told that baptism should happen after repentance and faith. Preaching to the crowd on the Day of Pentecost, Peter declared, *Repent and be baptised* (Acts 2:38). First repentance, then – and only then – baptism. When giving the disciples the Great Commission, Jesus told them, *Whoever believes and is baptised shall be saved* (Mark 16:16). Belief must precede baptism. They were to *make disciples of all nations, baptising them...* (Matthew 28:19). That is why when the Ethiopian eunuch asked Philip if he might be baptised, Philip replied, *If you believe with all your heart, you may* (Acts 8:36-37).

The scriptural conditions for baptism, then, are repentance, faith, and discipleship. This clearly rules out the possibility of babies being baptised, especially when we bear in mind that there is not one case of infant baptism to be found anywhere in the Bible. This leads us very understandably to ask the question, 'Then how did such an unscriptural practice ever come into existence, and why do those who claim to believe in the Bible persist in it today?'

Misunderstandings and the misuse of baptism

In seeking to answer this question we need to remember that the church of Jesus Christ has been in existence for nearly two thousand years and that during that time there has been plenty of opportunity for misunderstandings to arise and for unscriptural practices to creep in. In recent centuries God has been gradually drawing Christians back to the pattern of the early church and to the teachings of the scriptures. Yet for many there has been an unwillingness to abandon what has in some cases been the tradition of centuries, however unscriptural that tradition may be. Rather, such people have attempted to show that their traditions are scriptural, and as a result have *read into* the New Testament much that is not there. Such is unfortunately the case with the subject of infant baptism.

It seems that very early in the history of the church there arose the heresy of 'baptismal regeneration'. This theory taught that if you were not baptised you could not go to heaven, and that conversely if you were baptised you would go to heaven - or that you would at least stand a chance of getting there eventually! Now as Bible-believing Christians we know, of course, that it is by faith that we are saved (Galatians 2:16), and not by baptism. Baptism is an act of obedience because we are saved. It is not a ceremony to save us. Two cases in scripture make this point clear. In Acts 8 Simon the sorcerer was baptised (v.13) although his heart was not right before God (v.21), and in Luke 23:42-43 the repentant thief was obviously saved although he had no opportunity to be baptised.

Such scriptures conclusively demonstrate the error of the doctrine of 'baptismal regeneration', but it was from this error that the practice of infant baptism arose. Babies often died at an early age and the belief arose that if they were baptised they would go to heaven. That such an idea should be taken seriously is almost laughable to those who are familiar with the pages of the New Testament! It is utterly unthinkable that God would keep a baby out of heaven just because its parents didn't have it sprinkled! Jesus said concerning little children, *Of such is the kingdom of heaven*, and this is surely sufficient grounds for believing that babies (whether sprinkled or not) go straight to heaven when they die.

Finally, we should mention the question of household baptisms. Those who practise infant baptism usually try to justify it on the grounds that there are occasions in the Bible when whole households were baptised. It is probable, they say, that there were babies in those households. However, there is no evidence whatever that this was the case. There are five cases of household baptism in the New Testament, and not only are babies never mentioned, but if we look at each passage carefully we see that it is in fact highly unlikely that there were any in the households concerned.

In Acts 10:24-48 we read of the circumstances in which Cornelius and his household were baptised. In verse 24 we are told that he had called together his relatives and close friends. These people gathered *to listen to* what Peter had to say (v.33), were converted and received the Holy Spirit, speaking in other tongues (v.46). In verse 48 Peter commanded them to be baptised. It is possible that there were young children present, for young children may be saved and received the Holy Spirit, and for that matter may be baptised. But the circumstances described clearly rule out any possibility that tiny babies, who are incapable of repentance and faith, were converted, received the Holy Spirit, and were accordingly baptised in water.

Lydia and her household were baptised in Acts 16:14-15, but since she was probably single, having her own business, it seems unlikely that there were any babies in the home. The Philippian jailor and his household were baptised in Acts 16:32-34, but verse 34 tells us that the whole family *believed*, so clearly there were no babies present there, as babies are incapable of believing. The same is true of the household of Crispus (Acts 18:8). Paul baptised the household of Stephanas (1 Corinthians 1:16) but they are described as having devoted themselves to the service of the saints (1 Corinthians 16:15), a phrase which is hardly applicable to infants!

So we see that, far from strengthening the case of those who would seek to justify infant baptism, the examples of household baptism in the New Testament simple serve to show to what lengths people will go in an attempt to find in the scriptures a warrant for their unscriptural traditions and practices. A simple reading of the New Testament will leave us in no doubt that those who have repented of their sin and put their trust in Christ as Saviour, so becoming his disciples, are commanded to be immersed in water in the name of the Father and of the Son, and of the Holy Spirit (Matthew 28:19). Christians who have not been baptised in this way should seek to obey the Lord Jesus in this matter immediately.

QUESTIONS

1. READ John 12:26, 1 Peter 2:21

    What does Jesus command those who serve him?

    What did Christ do for us?

    What did he leave us?

    What should WE do?

2. READ Matthew 3:15

    Why didn't John want to baptise Jesus?

    What was Jesus' reply?

3. READ Matthew 28:19-20

    What was Jesus' last command to his disciples?

4. READ Romans 6:1-6

    To what are we dead and how did this happen?

    Into what are we baptised?

    What happens to the dead?

    Into what are we raised?

5. READ Matthew 3:6, Mark 1:5-9

    Where did John baptise?

6. READ John 3:23

    Why did John baptise at Aenon?

7. READ Acts 8:38

    Where did Philip and the eunuch both go?

8. What words in the scriptures mentioned in questions 5-7 show us that baptism is by immersion?

9. READ Acts 2:38, Mark 16:16, Matthew 28:19

   Which comes first, baptism or repentance?

   Which comes first, baptism or belief?

   Which comes first, baptism or becoming a disciple?

10. READ Acts 8:9-25, Luke 23:42-43

   How does Acts 8 show us that it is possible to be baptised and still not be right with God?

   How does Luke 23 show us that it is not necessary to be baptised to be saved?

CHAPTER FOURTEEN

Breaking of Bread

On the evening before his crucifixion the Lord Jesus gathered his disciples together in a large upper room where at his instructions Peter and John had already prepared the Passover meal. While they were eating, Jesus took bread, and having blessed it, he broke it and distributed it to his disciples. He then took wine, gave thanks for it, and the cup was passed from one to the other. Concerning the bread he said, *This is my body given for you; do this in remembrance of me.* Concerning the wine he said, *This cup is the new covenant in my blood, which is poured out for you* (Luke 22:19-20).

In simple obedience, the disciples ate the bread and drank the wine, and because he had told them to do so in remembrance of him, they continued to meet together for this purpose after his death. The observance came to be known as 'the breaking of bread' (Acts 2:42), 'the Lord's Supper' (1 Corinthians 11:20), and possibly 'the communion' (1 Corinthians 10:16, KJV). It has been practised in a variety of forms by the Christian Church ever since. It is one of the sad ironies of history, however, that the service which should demonstrate the unity of believers has been the point upon which the church has been most divided.

An examination of the various views is neither possible nor desirable within the scope of this book. The important thing is what the Bible teaches. We must not be content with the mere pronouncements and traditions of men; we must be satisfied only with the revelation of the Spirit of God himself through the pages of holy scripture. And as we examine the subject in the light of God's word, we discover the profound yet simple truth as to why the service was ordained, and as to how and when and by whom it should be observed.

Why it was ordained

As we have already seen, the communion service was ordained by the Lord Jesus as a memorial or reminder of his death (Luke 22:19-20, 1 Corinthians 11:24-25). But it is more than a reminder. It is also a proclamation. Paul tells us that as we eat the bread and drink the cup, we *proclaim the Lord's death until he comes* (1 Corinthians 11:26).

The word here translated *proclaim* is usually translated *preach* in other parts of the New Testament, and so we see that as we gather around the Lord's table there is a very real sense in which we are preaching Christ crucified as we partake of the bread and wine. In so doing we are reminding ourselves of the merits of his death, but we are also reminding *others*. We proclaim to our fellow-Christians and to those who are not yet Christians the importance of Jesus' death for us. And there is a sense in which we also proclaim to the principalities and powers in the heavenly realms the manifold wisdom of God demonstrated at Calvary!

But the Lord's supper is also the sign of a new covenant. In Jeremiah 31:31-34 God promised that he would make a new covenant with the people of God whereby he would write his law in their hearts. These verses are quoted in the New Testament in Hebrews 8:8-12 where the Holy Spirit makes clear that Jeremiah's prophecy was fulfilled in Christ.

In this connection we need to remember that the Lord's supper is the Christian counterpart of the Jewish Passover (Luke 22:15) and as we eat we are reminded that *Christ our Passover lamb has been sacrificed for us* (1 Corinthians 5:7). The Feast of the Passover was a memorial of God's covenant with the children of Israel (Exodus 12:14). The communion service is the memorial of the new covenant which was ratified by the shedding of the blood of Christ at Calvary (Matthew 26:28, 1 Corinthians 11:25). As we take the cup we are reminded that we have entered into covenant relationship with God almighty. 'From the least to the greatest' of us, we know the Lord; he is our God and we are his people; he forgives our wickedness and remembers our sins no more (Hebrews 8:10-12). What a covenant! What a privilege!

But that is not all. In breaking bread together we are not only proclaiming Christ crucified and reminding ourselves of the blessings of the New Covenant, we are also sharing in a great act of fellowship. The bread and the wine are the *communion* of the body and blood of Christ (1 Corinthians 10:16-17). The word 'communion' (Greek *koinonia*) conveys the idea of 'a sharing together in something with others'. The early disciples 'devoted themselves to the apostles' teaching and to fellowship (koinonia), to the breaking of bread and to prayer' (Acts 2:42).

The use of this word in the New Testament is a study in itself, revealing that the fellowship of the church is the joint participation in the blessings of Christ. The church is not just the sum total of individual Christians. It is a collective sharing in Christ. And as we break bread together we share collectively the benefits of his atoning death. We identify ourselves with the local assembly of believers and with that greater company which no one can number, the church universal, and with them rejoice in the blessings of Calvary. What a privilege it is to take communion. We remember and proclaim Jesus' death. We remind ourselves that we are God's covenant people. We collectively share in Christ himself.

How and when it should be observed

Although there are brief accounts of the last supper in the Gospels it is in 1 Corinthians 11 that we find the most complete explanation of the ordinance. As we examine the second half of this chapter we discover that the Lord's supper took place when they gathered as a church (v.18 cf. v.22). Of course there were no church buildings at the time, and we need to remember that the church is a body of people, not a building. This was a meal which believers shared when they came together as a church for worship and fellowship. This clearly distinguishes the Lord's supper from the ordinary meals which they ate at home (cf. vv 22 and 24), and the idea, current in some circles, that the breaking of bread is simply Christians having a meal together is, therefore, shown to be unscriptural.

However, it does appear that they did eat and drink rather more than is normal in a modern church communion service (v.21), but it should be noticed that Paul does not commend them for that! It is probable that the taking of the bread and wine formed a part of what was known as the *Agapé* or Love Feast, but this occasion was certainly not intended to be an excuse for eating or drinking too much (vv 21-22), nor was it merely to provide the fellowship which Christians enjoy when eating in one another's company. The specific purpose of the ordinance was the remembrance and proclamation of Christ's death (vv 24-26), self-examination (v.28) and fellowship (1 Corinthians 10:16-21).

In the early chapters of Acts it seems that this was taking place daily (Acts 2:42, 46), but later it appears that a weekly observance of the ordinance became customary (Acts 20:7). There is, however, no clear command in the New Testament as to how often we should break bread. We are simply told that when we do so we are to do so in remembrance of the Lord Jesus (1 Corinthians 11:25) and that we are expected to 'come together' specifically for this purpose (vv 18, 20). It is our privilege, but also our duty, to do so, in obedience to the command of our Lord Jesus Christ: *Do this.*

As we do so, we must examine ourselves lest we fail to discern *the Lord's body* (1 Corinthians 11:27-30). These verses undoubtedly refer to the matter of bad relationships with other Christians (already referred to in verse 18-22) who also form part of the body of Christ. If we are to avoid the judgment of the Lord we must judge ourselves. We must confess our sins to him and put right what is wrong so that we may eat of the bread and drink of the cup. As we do so, we do well in our thinking to look back to the cross in remembrance, to look up to the throne where Jesus reigns, and to look forward to his return, for the ordinance is *until he comes* (v.26).

Who may participate

In Acts 2:41-42 we read of those who devoted themselves to ... 'the breaking of bread'. These were those who had received the word and were baptised. On the basis of such verses some churches have precluded from the Lord's table fellow-Christians who have not been baptised, or who have not been baptised according to the traditions of their particular church. Some impose even more stringent conditions such as 'confirmation'.

In this connection, we need to remember, however, that when we believed in the Lord Jesus Christ we not only received eternal life (John 6:47) but in John 1:12 we are told that we 'received him'. Jesus also refers to this conversion experience of receiving him as *eating his flesh and drinking his blood* (John 6:54). It is clear from the context that these verses do not refer to the communion service, but are used metaphorically to refer to our receiving Christ as Saviour at conversion. It is at the communion service, however, that we remember how we have received Christ into our lives, how we have been made partakers of then divine nature, and by faith we feed on him who is the bread of life.

On these grounds, surely, it must be contended that all who have received Christ, whether baptised or not, may receive communion. However, it is difficult to understand how a person can wish to observe one of the ordinances of the Lord Jesus Christ without being willing to submit to the other! If we have received the word, let us be baptised. If we love him, we will keep his commandments. Baptism in water and attendance at the Lord's table are both commands of the Lord Jesus.

QUESTIONS

1. READ Luke 22:19-20

   What did Jesus say concerning the bread?

   What did Jesus say concerning the wine?

2. READ 1 Corinthians 11:24-26

   Why are we commanded to *do this?*

   What do we do whenever we eat the bread and drink the cup?

3. READ Jeremiah 31:31-34, Hebrews 8:8-12

   What did God promise to make with his people?

   Where would this be written?

   How does the new covenant compare with the old one?

4. READ Exodus 12:14, 1 Corinthians 5:7

   What was the Jewish Passover meant to be?

   Who is described as *our Passover lamb?*

5. READ Matthew 26:28, 1 Corinthians 11:25-30

   What is the communion service intended to be?

   What must we do at communion?

   What is the danger if we do not?

6. READ Acts 2:41-46, 20:7

   To what did they devote themselves?

   Who were those who did so?

   How often did they do so at first?

   How often did they do so later?

CHAPTER FIFTEEN

The Baptism with the Holy Spirit

Forty days after his resurrection, just before he ascended into heaven, Jesus gathered his disciples together and began to tell them something of the great task of world evangelism that lay before them. *You are to preach repentance and forgiveness of sins in my name,* he told them, *beginning at Jerusalem. But before you even start, you must wait in Jerusalem until you are clothed with power from on high* (Luke 24:47-49 paraphrased).

This power that he promised them was none other than the power of the Holy Spirit coming upon them (Acts 1:8) which would enable them to be witnesses for Christ to the ends of the earth. Jesus called it being *baptised with the Holy Spirit* (Acts 1:5). In obedience to his command that they should wait for this power, the disciples stayed in Jerusalem after Jesus' ascension into heaven, spending much time in prayer (Acts 1:14).

Finally, ten days later, on the Day of Pentecost they were all filled with the Holy Spirit and began to speak languages they had never learned as the Holy Spirit gave them the power to do so. After that they were a revolutionised group of people! The book of Acts tells us how they *turned the world upside down* (Acts 17:6, KJV). On the Day of Pentecost alone 3,000 people turned to Christ, and as the days went by multitudes continued to be added (Acts 2:41, 47; 4:4; 5:14; 6:7).

It is difficult to imagine what might have happened if the church had continued to move in the power of the Spirit down through the centuries of its history! Sadly, however, as the years went by, worldliness and materialism began to creep in, until not only was there little evidence of the power of the Spirit among so-called Christians, but for long centuries the gospel itself was scarcely preached. Of course, the Reformation began to change all that, but it was not until relatively recently that Christians all over the world began to realise that the power that was available to the early disciples on the Day of Pentecost is available to God's people today!

At first, at around about the beginning of the twentieth century, those Christians who began to believe this and who were 'baptised with the Holy Spirit' just like the early disciples, were misunderstood and often turned out of their churches and denominations. These people quite understandably began to meet together now that they were no longer welcome in their own churches, and so there came into being what has become known as the world-wide Pentecostal Movement.

The Pentecostal Movement has made rapid strides forward as Spirit-filled Christians have preached the Gospel in the power and demonstration of the Holy Spirit. As a result many Christians who worship in the churches and denominations which once rejected those who were baptised with the Holy Spirit, are themselves seeking and receiving this blessing.

Some are still sceptical. Others are interested, but not yet committed. Others are earnestly seeking. Some believe in the Baptism with the Holy Spirit, but do not believe that it is necessary to speak in tongues as the early disciples did. In fact some Christians are totally opposed to the Baptism with the Holy Spirit as Pentecostal Christians understand it. There is a great variety of views and interpretations, but if we will carefully and prayerfully examine the scriptures with an open mind we will not go astray.

What it is

When Jesus told his disciples that they would be *baptised with the Holy Spirit in a few days* (Acts 1:5), he also described what would happen as the Holy Spirit *coming upon* them (Acts 1:8). In Luke 24:49 he called it being *clothed with power from on high*. In the Old Testament we read that the Holy Spirit *came upon* Gideon (Judges 6:34) and again the word means *clothed.*

We saw when discussing the subject of water baptism, the literal meaning of *baptise* is *immerse*. So it is clear that the 'baptism' with the Holy Spirit is the Holy Spirit coming upon, covering, clothing, or immersing a person. When Jesus said that the disciples would be *baptised with* the Holy Spirit, and that the Holy Spirit would *come upon* them he was, therefore, saying the same thing. The baptism with the Holy Spirit is the Holy Spirit coming upon you.

When did it happen?

There are several occasions in the book of Acts when we read that the Holy Spirit came upon various people. It is from these passages that we may clearly see what happened when people received the Baptism with the Holy Spirit, what kind of people they were, and how and when they received it.

The first people to be baptised in the Holy Spirit in the Book of Acts were, of course, the disciples on the Day of Pentecost. In Acts 2:4 we are told that they were all *filled with* the Holy Spirit and began to speak in other tongues. Peter later described this as being *baptised with* the Holy Spirit (Acts 11:15-17), and told the questioning crowd that this was the Spirit being outpoured upon all people (Acts 2:17).

Now this can be understood in two different ways. It could mean that Pentecost was once and for all and that all mankind could ever expect to receive of the Holy Spirit was what happened at Pentecost. Alternatively it could mean that at Pentecost the Holy Spirit was so outpoured that he was, from that moment on, available for all people to receive if they would repent and believe the gospel.

This is obviously the correct interpretation because there are passages in the Book of Acts where we see that the experience of Pentecost was repeated on several occasions. At Pentecost the Spirit was outpoured. He came upon the one hundred and twenty disciples in the upper room. But when Peter says that the Spirit is outpoured upon all people, he is telling his hearers that the Spirit will come upon them too (Acts 2:38-39).

Some time later, the apostles heard that many of the Samaritans had been converted under Philip's ministry. They had not yet, however, had the Spirit come upon them (Acts 8:16). So the apostles sent Peter and John in order that the Samaritans might 'receive the Holy Spirit' (another scriptural expression for receiving the Baptism in the Holy Spirit – Acts 8:15).

In Acts 10:44-48 we read how the Holy Spirit came on the Roman centurion Cornelius and his household and in Acts 11:15-16 Peter describes this as the Baptism in the Holy Spirit. The other expressions used in these passages are also interesting, for what Peter calls being 'baptised in the Holy Spirit' in Acts 11:16 is referred to in Acts 10 as

> The Spirit coming on Cornelius (10:44)

> The gift of the Holy Spirit being poured out (10:45)

> Receiving the Holy Spirit (10:47).

In Acts 19:6 the Holy Spirit also came on the Ephesian disciples who had not yet 'received' him (19:2), and we notice that, like the Samaritans in Acts 8, they received through the laying on of hands.

There are then at least four occasions in the book of Acts when we read that the Holy Spirit *came on* people. In these passages we are given a more or less complete account of what happened when people were baptised in the Spirit in fulfilment of Jesus' promise in Acts 1:5-8.

We must now look at each of these four instances in more detail and ask:

> To whom was the Baptism in the Holy Spirit given?

> When did they receive it?

> What happened when they received it?

Answering questions like these we will assure ourselves of the scriptural truth of this very important subject. Since the Book of Acts, like the rest of Scripture, is useful for doctrine (2 Timothy 3:16), we need to realise that the experiences that the early church received may be received by the church today. The blessings individual Christians experienced in New Testament times are available to us as individual Christians today. We may experience in our own lives the very same power that transformed the spiritual experience of men like Peter and Paul! To be sure about this, we will now seek to answer the question, 'To whom is the Baptism in the Holy Spirit promised?'

To whom is it promised?

In Acts 1:5 when Jesus told his disciples that in a few days they would be baptised with the Holy Spirit, he also described the experience as (literally) *the promise of the Father* (Acts 1:4, Luke 24:49) which NIV paraphrases as *the gift my Father promised.* The outpouring of the Spirit on the Day of Pentecost was the fulfilment of what God had promised through the prophet Joel centuries before (Acts 2:16-17, Joel 2:28-32). This promise of the Father was the baptism in the Holy Spirit, the Spirit outpoured upon all people. Preaching to the crowd that gathered at Pentecost, Peter said that this promise was

For you, for your children, for all who are far off, for all whom the Lord our God will call (Acts 2:38-39).

This verse makes it clear that the promise of the Father, the baptism with the Holy Spirit, is available to all Christians, indeed to all people if they will repent and believe the gospel.

When should it be received?

When the apostles at Jerusalem heard that Samaria had received the word of God the very first thing they did was to send Peter and John in order that the Samaritan converts might receive the Holy Spirit through the laying on of hands (Acts 8:14-17).

Similarly, the very first question that Paul asked when he found a group of disciples at Ephesus was *Did you receive the Holy Spirit when you believed?* (Acts 19:2).

In the case of Cornelius and his household (Acts 10:44-48) the Holy Spirit fell on them before Peter had finished preaching. They had only just heard the gospel. They had had no opportunity to make any outward expression of their acceptance of it. They had certainly not yet been baptised in water. But they were wonderfully baptised in the Holy Spirit!

In fact it is noteworthy that, after the outpouring of the Spirit on the Day of Pentecost, the Spirit was received at, or immediately after, conversion. The normal scriptural pattern seems to be:

Repentance and faith (conversion)
Water baptism
Baptism in the Holy Spirit

All these were expected to occur very close together as Peter's exhortation in Acts 2:38 implies:

Repent and be baptised, every one of you... and you will receive the gift of the Holy Spirit.

The reason that the disciples were commanded to wait in Acts 1:4 is simply that until Pentecost the promise of the outpouring of the Spirit had not yet been fulfilled. They had to wait for its fulfilment. But once the Father's promise through the prophet had been fulfilled (Acts 2:17) the gift became available to all who would repent and be baptised (Acts 2:38-39).

This does not mean that the Baptism with the Holy Spirit is conversion, or that one receives it automatically when one is baptised in water. (The experience of the Samaritans and Ephesians makes that clear – Acts 8:12-17, 19:1-7). The work of the Spirit at conversion is one of convicting and regenerating. The work of the Spirit at the Baptism with the Spirit is clothing with power. The work of the Spirit at conversion *comes before* water baptism. The Baptism with the Spirit usually *follows* it. The Baptism with the Spirit is often accompanied with the laying on of hands, and always with certain supernatural manifestations, neither of which have any connection with his work at conversion.

Conversion and the Baptism with the Spirit are, therefore, clearly distinct, but that does not alter the fact that all Christians should seek to be baptised with water and with the Holy Spirit immediately after they are converted.

What happens when we receive it?

The Bible is our sole authority for doctrine. This means that all that we believe, including our teaching about the Baptism with the Spirit, must be based upon the scriptures. So, what we believe about what happens when a person is baptised in the Holy Spirit must be taken from the scriptures and from the scriptures alone.

In these days millions of people are being baptised in the Spirit all over the world. So it's not surprising that there are a number of different views on this important matter. The danger is that, as a result of a wonderful experience, people start to build a doctrine on that experience. However, as we examine the word of God, we discover that there was only one recurring phenomenon that was invariably accepted as the sign that the Spirit had come. There were sometimes other signs as well, but only one was repeated on each occasion and that was speaking in tongues.

On the Day of Pentecost (Acts 2:1-4) there was the sound of a violent wind; there were tongues of fire that sat on each of them; but this was before they were all filled with the Spirit. What happened as a result of their being filled was that *they began to speak in other tongues.*

When Cornelius was baptised in the Spirit, Peter said that the Holy Spirit *came on them as on us at the beginning* (Acts 11:15). What had convinced him about this was not the repetition of the wind or fire – for there was no such repetition – but the fact that Cornelius and his household were heard to *speak with tongues and magnify God* (Acts 10:46) as the first disciples had on the Day of Pentecost.

Similarly, when the Spirit came upon the Ephesians (Acts 19:6), *they spoke in tongues and prophesied.* It is interesting that tongues is mentioned before prophecy here. Prophecy is the greater gift (1 Corinthians 14:5) and we might have expected it to be mentioned first. So why is tongues mentioned first? Presumably because it happened first.

So, in the book of Acts, whenever people experienced the power of the Spirit coming upon them, the very first thing that happened was that they began to speak a language that they had never learned – they began to speak in tongues.

It is true that there is no mention of tongues in the case of the Samaritans in Acts 8; but we are told that Simon *saw* something happen when they received the Spirit. It would obviously have been something supernatural for a sorcerer to have offered money to gain possession of it, and commentators are generally agreed that what he saw was speaking in tongues.

Besides, the fact that what Simon saw is not mentioned shows that Acts 8 is not a full description of what took place. What we can therefore categorically state is this:

Whenever there is a full description of the Baptism in the Spirit in the Book of Acts it is accompanied by speaking in tongues.

If that was the normal pattern for believers then, we must surely teach it as the norm for today.

Conclusion

The Baptism with the Holy Spirit is the Spirit coming upon a Christian giving power for service. There are four main passages in Acts which describe this taking place. From these we learn that, once the Spirit had been outpoured at Pentecost, the blessing was given to young converts usually immediately after their baptism in water. The experience was sometimes received through the laying on of hands and was accompanied by speaking in tongues.

In recent years millions of Christians have been baptised in the Spirit in this way. Have you?

QUESTIONS

1. READ Acts 1:4-5, 8

    How is the gift promised by the Father (v.4) described in v.5?

    How is this described in verse 8?

    What would they be as a result of receiving this?

2. READ Acts 2:1-4, 17, 38-39

    Who were the first people to be baptised with the Holy Spirit?

    How is this described in v. 4?

    How is this described in v.17?

    To whom is the promise of the Spirit made in vv. 38-39?

3. READ Acts 8:5-17

    Why did the apostles in Jerusalem send Peter and John to Samaria (v.14)?

    Had the Samaritans already believed?

    Had they been baptised?

    Were they yet baptised in the Spirit?

    How did they receive the Spirit (v.17)?

4. READ Acts 10:44-48, 11:15-17

    How did the Jews know that the Gentiles had received the Spirit?

    How did Peter later describe what happened?

5. READ Acts 19:1-7

    What was the first question that Paul asked these disciples?

    Whose baptism had they already received?

    In whose name did Paul baptise them in water?

    When did the Holy Spirit come upon them?

    What happened when the Spirit came upon them?

6. READ Acts 2:4, 10:46, 19:6

    What was the first thing that happened immediately after these people were baptised in the Spirit?

CHAPTER SIXTEEN

The Gifts of the Holy Spirit

The outpouring of the Spirit which took place at the beginning of the twentieth century was marked by two things. There was, as we have seen, a realisation that the Baptism with the Holy Spirit was available to Christians today as an enduement with power from on high. With that realisation, however, there came also the understanding that the supernatural gifts of the Spirit seen in operation in the Acts of the Apostles and referred to in 1 Corinthians 12-14 might be received and exercised in our present generation. Indeed, what singles out the present-day Pentecostal Movement from all the revivals of charismatic phenomena in church history is the emphasis placed upon the biblical connection between the Baptism with the Holy Spirit and the supernatural sign-gift of tongues.

The Baptism with the Spirit, although a wonderful experience in itself, is not essentially a goal but a gateway. Through it we have entered into an entirely new realm – the realm of the supernatural. It is important, therefore, that we should know not only what the gifts of the Spirit are, but also what they are for and how we may receive them.

What they are

In 1 Corinthians 12:1 Paul tells us that we are not to be ignorant about spiritual gifts. He then lists in verses 8-10 the following nine gifts:

The message of wisdom, the message of knowledge, faith, gifts of healing, miraculous powers, prophecy, the ability to distinguish between spirits, tongues, and the interpretation of tongues.

It would not be possible within the scope of this brief chapter to give a detailed definition of each of the gifts mentioned. There are plenty of books which specialise on this subject readily available. For our purpose it will be sufficient to outline what the scriptures teach concerning the gifts of the Spirit as a whole.

The first thing to notice is that they are **gifts**. The Greek word used here is *charisma* (plural *charismata*) from which of course we get our word 'charismatic'. The word *charisma* comes in turn from another Greek word, *charis* which means 'grace'. From this we see that the basic idea behind these gifts is that they are given to us because of God's grace. Like the gift *(charisma)* of eternal life (Romans 6:23), spiritual gifts cannot be earned by human merit, but must be received in gratitude and dependence on the grace of God.

Another important aspect of these gifts is that they are **supernatural**. Some gifts which God gives us are clearly natural (as in 1 Corinthians 7:7 for example), but these gifts are described as 'spiritual' (Greek *pneumatika*). They are the kind of gifts to which the writer to the Hebrews is referring when he speaks of signs, wonders, and... miracles, and gifts of the Holy Spirit distributed according to his will (Hebrews 2:4).

The context here puts the gifts of the Spirit in the same category as signs and wonders and miracles. Speaking in tongues, for example, has nothing to do with the ability to learn foreign languages quickly at school! It is the ability to speak a foreign language although you have never learnt it (Acts 2:4ff).

Finally, we notice that spiritual gifts are described as **manifestations** of the Spirit (1 Corinthians 12:7). This word means 'the outward evidence of an inner principle'. So the gifts of the Spirit are an outward evidence of the power of the Holy Spirit working within us. A person may speak a language that they have never learned because the Holy Spirit, who knows all things, dwells within them. We can work miracles because the all-powerful God lives inside us!

Of course, not all supernatural manifestations come from God. Satan has his miracle-workers too! The miraculous events, which take place in a spiritualist s¾ance, the messages from the ouija board, the supernatural powers of the mystical eastern religions, the practices of witchcraft and Satanism, are not from heaven! Their miracle-gifts come from a variety of evil spirits. The gifts God gives come from the one, same, Holy Spirit (1 Corinthians 12:4-11). The evil spirits never call Jesus Lord. People controlled by the Holy Spirit will gladly acknowledge his Lordship (1 Corinthians 12:3). The demons only curse his name.

What they are for

The major purpose of the Baptism with the Holy Spirit is that the believer might be empowered to be a witness for Jesus (Acts 1:8). One of the ways in which this power is evidenced in evangelism is through the supernatural gifts the Spirit gives. Jesus promised that miraculous signs would accompany the preaching of the gospel and that in this way God would confirm his word (Mark 16:15-20). This is backed up by Hebrews 2:4 which tells us that God testified to the message of salvation preached by the early disciples *by signs, wonders and... miracles, and gifts of the Holy Spirit.*

Paul, too, could talk of how he had been used to lead the Gentiles to obey God by what he had said and done, *by the power of signs and miracles through the power of the Spirit* as he had fully proclaimed the gospel of Christ (Romans 15:18-19). Surely we need to pray like the early church that signs and wonders might be done in the name of Jesus and that God's servants might preach his word with boldness (Acts 4:29-31).

So the gifts of the Spirit are certainly of use in evangelism. However, they are also of use for the edification of the local church. (Truly scriptural evangelism does not just win people for Jesus; it establishes churches). By the time Paul wrote to the church at Rome it was already a large and important one, yet he longed to see them in order that he might impart to them some spiritual gift to make them strong (Romans 1:11). Writing to the Corinthians about spiritual gifts he says everything must be done for the strengthening of the church (1 Corinthians 14:5). If we eagerly desire spiritual gifts – and Paul says we should – we must try to *excel in gifts that build up the church* (1 Corinthians 14:12). So the two main purposes of spiritual gifts are evangelism and the edification of the church.

How we may receive them

Since the gifts of the Spirit are so important we need to understand what the scriptures teach about how they may be received. In this connection we need to remember that it is the Spirit who distributes the gifts to each person just as he, the Spirit, determines (1 Corinthians 12:11). Ultimately it is God who decides what gifts he gives us. At the same time, God tells us to desire them eagerly (1 Corinthians 12:31, 14:1, 12). The Greek word used on each of these three occasions means literally *to strive fervently after.*

God will decide what gifts he will give us, but at the same time he encourages to strive fervently after them! In the realm of the spiritual God commands us to do the very thing that in the realm of the natural he forbids. Exodus 20:17 tells us that we may not covet material things – our neighbour's house, wife, servant, ox or ass. But we are to covet spiritual gifts. It seem very significant that in those parts of the world where materialism is least in evidence, the gifts of the Spirit are most in evidence in the church. If we were to spend less time in the pursuit of material gain and were to devote more of our attention to the things of the Spirit, we would come closer to seeing the revival we undoubtedly need!

Once we start to desire spiritual gifts, we should pray for them. The speaker in tongues, for example, is told to pray that he may interpret (1 Corinthians 14:13). Of course, when we pray, we should always pray in faith (James 1:6). When the gifts are used in the context of evangelism they are promised to 'those who believe' (Mark 16:17-18), and anyone who prophesies must do so 'in proportion to his faith' (Romans 12:6). We must *desire* the gifts, *ask for* the gifts, and *believe for* the gifts.

May God raise up from among us men and women, filled with the Holy Spirit, exercising the mighty gifts of the Spirit, preaching the word in the power and demonstration of the Spirit, so that our evangelism might be effective, and our churches established and edified.

QUESTIONS

1. READ 1 Corinthians 12:1

   What word is used in this verse to describe the gifts Paul is talking about?

2. READ 1 Corinthians 12:8-10

   What gifts of the Spirit are listed here?

3. READ Hebrews 2:4

   What words show us that the gifts of the Spirit are supernatural?

4. READ 1 Corinthians 12:7

   What word is used here to show that spiritual gifts are the outward evidence of the Spirit working within us?

5. READ 1 Corinthians 12:1-11

   What will a person who speaks by the power of the Holy Spirit gladly acknowledge?

   How many gifts are listed in this passage?

   Are these given by one Spirit or by many spirits?

6. READ Mark 16:15-20, Hebrews 2:4, Romans 15:18-19

   What has God promised will accompany the preaching of his word?

   With what did God bear witness to the testimony of the early disciples?

   As Paul preached the gospel, how did God bring the Gentiles to obedience?

7. READ 1 Corinthians 12:11

   Who distributes the gifts?

   Who makes the decision about who has which?

8. READ 1 Corinthians 14:5, 12, 26

   Why is one gift greater than another here?

   What should be our motive in seeking the gifts?

   When the church gathers, with what purpose is everything to be done?

9. READ 1 Corinthians 12:31, 14:1, 12-13
    What does God tell us to do concerning the gifts?
    How may the gift of interpretation of tongues be received?
10. READ James 1:6, Romans 12:6
    When we pray, what is essential?
    When we prophesy, how do we do so?

CHAPTER SEVENTEEN

The Gifts of Christ

In the last chapter we considered the list of spiritual gifts found in 1 Corinthians 12:8-10. We now turn our attention to another list. This is found in Ephesians 4:11 and is also of great importance to the church of Jesus Christ today

. The list includes *apostles, prophets, evangelists, pastors and teachers* and reveals the variety of leadership gifts that God has set in the church. In this chapter we will examine the nature, purpose, and importance of these leadership gifts.

The nature of the leadership gifts

Before considering briefly the nature of each of these ministries it will be helpful to notice two basic differences between the leadership gifts of Ephesians 4:11 and the spiritual gifts referred to in 1 Corinthians 12.

First, leadership gifts are said to be given by *Christ* (Ephesians 4:7), whereas spiritual gifts are given by *the Holy Spirit* (1 Corinthians 12:8).

Secondly, spiritual gifts are given to individuals for the benefit and edification of the church (1 Corinthians 12:7, 11-13, 14:12), whereas leadership gifts are not so much given to individuals, but *are* individuals given to the church (Ephesians 4:11-12). Paul, for example, did not, strictly speaking, *have* the gift of apostleship. Paul himself *was* the gift. He was given to the church as an apostle.

With this distinction in mind, let us now proceed to consider each of the gifts mentioned.

Apostles

Basically the word 'apostle' means *one who has been sent*. The Greek verb *apostello* (from which it comes) is used frequently in the New Testament in a perfectly ordinary way to mean 'send' (as when Pilate's wife sent a message to him in

Matthew 27:19). In its more specialised sense, however, the word was used to refer first to the twelve men Jesus chose to be with him and to send out to preach and heal (Mark 3:14-15). Then it refers to a wider circle of people the church recognised as having this particular ministry. Paul and Barnabas are obvious examples of apostles in this wider group (Acts 14:14).

At first, an apostle was one who had seen the risen Christ and who was sent out by him to be a witness of the resurrection (Acts 1:21-22). Apostleship was attested by the supernatural gifts as well as the fruit of the Spirit (2 Corinthians 12:12) and, in the case of Paul at least, involved planting churches as we see from the Book of Acts.

Some have argued that the leadership gift of apostle was not intended to continue beyond the period of the early church, on the grounds that to be an apostle one was expected to have 'seen the Lord'. However, the fact that the early Christians required this as one of the qualifications of apostleship in no way suggests that they would have expected it of the apostles of later generations!

Indeed, several facts indicate that this important ministry was intended to continue:

the New Testament refers to several apostles other than the original twelve

nowhere does it state that the gift was to be withdrawn

in fact it states that the gift is needed to prepare God's people for works of service (Ephesians 4:11-12)

down through church history, and in our own generation God has clearly given people this ministry.

These facts provide sufficient grounds for believing that the ascended Christ is still giving some to be apostles *to prepare God's people for works of service so that the body of Christ may be built up.*

Prophets

When considering the ministry of the prophet it is helpful to remember the distinction which we have already made between leadership gifts and spiritual gifts. In this way we will not confuse the spiritual gift of prophecy with the ministry of the prophet. Undoubtedly all prophets prophesy. But not all those who exercise the gift of prophecy are prophets in the Ephesians 4:11 sense. To have received a *spiritual* gift does not necessarily imply that one has received a *leadership* gift.

The word 'prophesy' means 'to speak on behalf of' and clearly both those who are prophets (in the leadership-gift sense) and those who have the spiritual gift of prophecy 'speak on behalf of' God to his people. The spiritual gift, however, is essentially for the *strengthening, encouragement and comfort* of the church (1 Corinthians 14:3), and we are all encouraged to desire it eagerly (1 Corinthians 14:39), whereas the leadership gift of prophet would seem to include an element of revelation (e.g. Agabus, Acts 11:27-28, 21:10-11), and not all Christians would expect to have it (1 Corinthians 12:29).

Yet, having distinguished the spiritual gift from the leadership gift, we must acknowledge that there is a connection between them. Indeed, it is difficult to know whether the prophets referred to in 1 Corinthians 14:29-32 are leadership gifts or simply those who exercise the spiritual gift. The context certainly seems to imply the latter.

However, asking whether a person has the leadership gift of a prophet or exercises the spiritual gift of prophecy can be an unproductive exercise! What is really important is weighing carefully what they say (1 Corinthians 14:29). God does speak to his people by the direct revelation of his Spirit and we need to pay attention!

Evangelists

Considering the prominence that is given to the ministry of the evangelist in the work of the church today it is surprising to discover that in the whole of the New Testament only one person is specifically named as being one.

We are told that Philip, who had been one of the seven people appointed to wait on tables in Acts 6, was an evangelist (Acts 21:8). His ministry is vividly described for us in Acts 8, where we read of his visit to Samaria and of his leading the Ethiopian eunuch to Christ. We see that his message was very simple. He preached Christ (v.5). He preached Jesus (v.35). His message was confirmed with signs and wonders (vv.6-7). When people believed his message, they were baptised by immersion in water (vv.12, 38-39). Although he himself was very much led by the Spirit (vv.29, 39), his ministry in itself was not sufficient for the young converts. He does not seem to have possessed the specialised ministry of laying hands on people to receive the Baptism in the Holy Spirit, so the apostles sent Peter and John to help in this connection.

It is important to realise that no one ministry is sufficient for all the needs of God's people. We need apostles *and* prophets *and* evangelists *and* pastors *and* teachers! Young Christians need to be careful that the more spectacular ministry of the evangelist does not detract from the authority and ministry of their pastor(s).

Pastors and Teachers

In the Greek language in which the New Testament was first written, the word *poimen* (translated 'pastor' in Ephesians 4:11) is usually translated 'shepherd'. Such scriptures as Acts 20:28 and 1 Peter 5:2 show clearly that those who were to shepherd and feed the flock were usually referred to as 'elders' or 'overseers' and the qualifications for holding such an office in the local church are listed in 1 Timothy 3 and Titus 1. One such qualification was that the elder must be *able to teach* (1 Timothy 3:2, Titus 1:9).

As far as the New Testament is concerned, therefore, a person cannot be a pastor unless they are able to teach. This is why I have included *teachers* along with *pastors* in the heading for this section. Indeed the Greek text of Ephesians 4:11 can be understood to mean that the two words refer to the same leadership gift. However, perhaps we could say that although a pastor needs to be a teacher, a teacher need not necessarily be a pastor, as a teacher might have an itinerant ministry.

A detailed study of the privileges and responsibilities of local church leadership is not possible within the scope of this book. Perhaps it is sufficient to say that those to whom God has given the serious responsibility of shepherding and feeding his sheep deserve the respect and allegiance of those they are called to lead.

The purpose and importance of the leadership gifts

As we read on in Ephesians 4 and consider the purposes for which these gifts have been given to the church, we realise something of their tremendous importance. In a day when much emphasis has been placed on the renewal of the *spiritual* gifts in the church, it is vital that we realise that whatever gifts of the Spirit we may exercise, we still need the *leadership* gifts that God gives to his church. As individual Christians, and as churches, we still need apostles, prophets, evangelists, pastors and teachers

that God's people will be equipped to do better work for him, building up the church, the body of Christ, to a position of strength and maturity, until finally we all believe alike about our salvation and about our Saviour, God's Son, and all become full-grown in the Lord – yes to the point of being filled full with Christ (Ephesians 4:12-13, Living Bible).

We should pray that God might increasingly raise up these ministries among us. We should submit ourselves to those God has set in office in his church. We should search our hearts to see if perhaps God has gifted us and is calling us to one of these important areas of service for him.

QUESTIONS

1. READ Ephesians 4:7-12, 1 Corinthians 12:7-13, 14:12

    Who are the leadership gifts?

    Who is said to give the leadership gifts?

2. To whom are spiritual gifts given and for whose benefit?

    Who is said to give spiritual gifts?

3. READ Mark 3:14-19, Acts 14:14

    What were the first apostles sent out to do?

    Which two apostles were not part of the original group?

4. READ 1 Corinthians 14:3, 39; 12:29

    What is the purpose of the gift of prophecy?

    Who is encouraged to be eager to prophesy?

    Can all Christians expect to be prophets?

5. READ Acts 8:5-7, 35, 21:8

    Who is at the centre of the evangelist's message?

    With what was the evangelist's message confirmed?

    Who is named as an evangelist in the New Testament?

6. READ Acts 20:28, 1 Peter 5:1-2

    Who has the responsibility to shepherd the flock in these verses?

    How is their job described?

7. READ Hebrews 13:17

    What is the responsibility of church leaders?

    What should be the attitude of the church members?

8. READ Ephesians 4:11-13

    For what purpose have these leadership gifts been given to the church?

CHAPTER EIGHTEEN

Divine Healing

One of the most notable features of the outpouring of the Holy Spirit that took place in the twentieth century was that, along with the belief in the supernatural baptism and gifts of the Spirit, there came a resurgence of faith in God's power and willingness to heal the sick miraculously.

As a result amazing miracles have taken place and many have been wonderfully healed by the power of God. The subject, however, is not without its problems and, sadly, in some quarters, even abuses. It is therefore very important that we should know what we believe about healing and why we believe it.

A right understanding of divine healing

As evidence for the fact that the healing of our sicknesses is the privilege of the people of God we may point first to God's promise in Exodus 15:26. Israel had been brought out of Egypt by a supernatural act of divine deliverance. The Egyptians had perished beneath the waters of the Red Sea. As a further token of his mighty power the Lord had made sweet the bitter waters of Marah (Exodus 15:23-25). God was showing his people that he was able to meet all their needs. Then came the reassuring promise:

If you listen carefully to the voice of the Lord your God, and do what is right in his eyes... I will not bring on you any of the diseases I brought on the Egyptians; for I am the Lord who heals you.

The fact that there were those who did not meet the conditions of the promise, and who were therefore unable to avail themselves of God's gracious provision of healing, in no way invalidates the promise. It rather confirms it. It was God's will for his people to be healthy. Sickness was a curse which resulted from disobedience (Deuteronomy 28:59-61).

God's willingness to heal is also confirmed by the fact that our Lord Jesus Christ *went around doing good and healing all who were under the devil's power* (Acts 10:38). The Gospels provide many examples of this (Matthew 4:23-24, 8:16, 9:35, Mark 6:56, Luke 6:17-19, for example).

When Jesus sent his disciples out to preach he commanded them to *cure every kind of disease and sickness* (Matthew 10:1, 7-8). And this commission to heal was not limited to the time of his earthly ministry. In his final words to his disciples before his ascension Jesus commanded his disciples to go into all the world and preach the gospel. Those who believed would cast out demons, speak with new tongues and heal the sick in his name (Mark 16:15-20).

The fact that they did so is well illustrated in the book of Acts. In Acts 3:7-9 a lame man was healed in the name of Jesus resulting in the salvation of thousands of people (Acts 4:4). In Acts 4:30 the early church prayed that God would stretch out his hand to heal in the name of Jesus. In Acts 5:14-16 multitudes were healed in the streets of Jerusalem. Miracles were performed in the ministry of Stephen (Acts 6:8) and the sick were healed as Philip preached the gospel to the Samaritans (Acts 8:6-8). Peter was used to heal the sick and to raise the dead in Acts 9:33-42. At Paul's command a cripple leapt to his feet and walked (Acts 14:8-10), diseases departed (Acts 19:12) and the dead were raised (Acts 20:9-12). And it does not seem that the power to heal was ever withdrawn, for in the very last chapter of Acts the sick are still being healed (Acts 28:8-9), and in James 5:14-16 explicit instructions are given to Christians who need healing.

In both Old and New Testaments, then, we see God's power and willingness to heal his people. As we saw in an earlier chapter, when God made man he made him perfect and put him in a perfect creation. Everything God made was 'very good' (Genesis 1:31). It is clear that man was not only morally, but also physically perfect. There was no sickness in the Garden of Eden. There is to be no sickness in heaven (Revelation 21:4). The existence of sickness is the result of

Adam's sin. The whole of creation was affected by the Fall (Romans 8:22).

But just as God has not left us without a ransom for sin, so too he has not left us without a remedy for sickness. By Christ's atoning death on the cross he has reconciled to God all those who believe. By faith in the substitutionary sacrifice offered at Calvary repentant sinners are brought into right relationship with God. Their sins are washed away. The effects of the Fall are counteracted. Sin, the root cause of sickness is atoned for. By restoring us to fellowship with our Maker, Christ has, by his death, made provision for the healing of our bodies.

It is in this sense that healing may be rightly said to be 'in the atonement'. Of course, the word 'atonement' by its very meaning essentially refers to sin (see Chapter Four). Because of the atonement we are redeemed, we are reconciled to God, we are no longer enemies but sons. And the blessings of the New Testament are no less than those of the Old. To those who are by covenant his people, God still says, *I am the Lord who heals you.*

The right use of divine healing

As we examine the New Testament we discover that there are two main forms of divine healing. They are distinct, both in the purpose for which they are given and in the manner in which they are received, although there are, by the very nature of the case, many similarities between them. First there is healing for the believer. This is described in James 5:14-16. Then there is healing for the unbeliever. This operates in the context of evangelism and is referred to in Mark 16:16-20 and in the various examples in Acts we mentioned earlier.

Concerning the latter, it is clear that the Lord Jesus promised that miraculous healing would be one of the signs by which he would confirm the word of those who preach the gospel. In this connection it should be noted that healing was to *accompany* the preaching of the gospel. The apostolic message was *Christ died for our sins* (1 Corinthians 15:1-4). That is what they preached. They did not preach healing. They *did* it!

Notice too that in Mark 16 it is the one who is laying hands on the sick who appears to be responsible for exercising faith (vv. 17-18), not the sick person who may well still be an unbeliever.

Further, it needs to be pointed out that these verses do not imply that all who have hands laid on them will be miraculously healed. Jesus was not saying that every believer would be used in healing or that every sick person would be healed. What he does promise is that he will confirm his word by working in a variety of ways, including miraculous healing, to authenticate the message of the gospel to the unconverted. Perhaps if this were borne in mind, and if a greater emphasis were placed on the leading of the Spirit in the matter of praying for the sick, there would be less apparent 'failures' in the ministry of modern evangelists.

The problem would also be helped considerably if believers would remember that the form of healing prescribed for them is not that to be found in Mark 16, but rather that of James 5. The believer who is 'in trouble' (literally *suffering evil*) is to pray for himself (v.13). If he is sick, he is to call for the elders of the church who should pray in faith in the name of the Lord, anointing the sick person with oil.

James encourages Christians to pray for one another that they might be healed, and where applicable, to confess their faults to one another. Healing is promised, though not necessarily instantaneously. We sometimes need to persist in prayer. The conditions which govern all types of prayer are surely applicable in this context too. (The end of James 4 makes it clear that we cannot even be sure that we will be alive tomorrow – unless it is God's will!) Finally, it would seem sensible, and biblical, that when God has provided a simple natural remedy for a sickness, Christians should thankfully avail themselves of it.

Some problems of divine healing

The basic problem that lies at the heart of most questions that arise about the doctrine of healing is the simple fact that not everybody is healed. Pastors who have watched the suffering of some of the greatest saints in their congregation simply cannot believe that the answer is merely a matter of sin or unbelief on the part of the sufferer. The scriptures themselves do not support this suggestion.

We need to remember that even in Bible times there is evidence that there were occasions when not everyone was healed. Of course, there were times when everyone was, especially during the ministry of the Lord Jesus, from which we may conclude that we may well expect special periods of divine visitation when the same could happen again, as it did for the early Christians in Acts 5:16. But nowhere else in Acts are we told that such a thing took place. In fact, even in the ministry of the Lord Jesus there was at least one occasion when only one out of a large crowd was healed (John 5:1-9). And those who remind us of the health and strength of Moses whose eyesight was still good even at the age of one hundred and twenty usually fail to mention Isaac who died blind!

To attempt to deal with the problems of healing at all is a formidable task. To seek to do so within the scope of so brief a chapter is an impossibility. Perhaps we do well to remember as we consider the problem of those who are not yet healed that the spirit is more important than the body, that God does chastise us that we might be partakers of his holiness, that Paul's thorn – whatever it was – was in his flesh, and that he did leave Trophimus at Miletus sick.

As Christians we are still living in a world that is under the curse. The whole creation is groaning as in the pains of childbirth (Romans 8:22) and we ourselves groan inwardly waiting for the redemption of the body (v.23). But the day is coming when the creation itself will be delivered from its bondage to decay into the glorious freedom of the children of God! There's going to be a resurrection. We shall receive a body 'like his glorious body'. Our mortal bodies will be clothed with immortality! Death itself will be swallowed up in victory (1 Corinthians 15:50ff). Then every promise of healing will be fulfilled, for there will be no more death or mourning or crying or pain, for the old order of things will have passed away (Revelation 21:4).

QUESTIONS

1. READ Exodus 15:26

   What is God's clear command to his people?

   What is God's clear promise to his people?

2. READ Acts 10:38

   How is God's willingness to heal shown in the ministry of the Lord Jesus?

3. READ Matthew 4:23-24, 8:16, 9:35, Mark 6:56, Luke 6:17-19

   The above scriptures describe the healing ministry of the Lord Jesus. In each of the passages listed there is ONE word that indicates the scale on which he healed. What is it?

4. READ Matthew 10:1-8, Mark 16:16-20

   What was Jesus command to his disciples?

   What promises are made to those who preach the gospel?

   Who is responsible for laying hands on the sick?

   Who is responsible for exercising faith?

   How were the promises in 4b fulfilled in Acts? See Acts 3:7-9; 4:30; 5:14-16; 6:8; 8:6-8; 9:33-42; 19:12; 20:9-12.

5. READ James 5:14-16

   What instructions are given to Christians who are sick?

   Whose responsibility is it to pray in faith?

   What does the Lord promise to do?

6. READ Romans 8:18-27

   What encouragement do these verses offer to Christians who have not yet been healed?

CHAPTER NINETEEN

Holiness

The subject of holiness is possibly one of the most difficult doctrines in the Bible. It has certainly been the cause of great disagreement between Christians in the past, and is still the source of much misunderstanding among Christians today. Nevertheless, whatever the difficulties may be, the Bible clearly teaches that we are to be holy for the simple reason that God is holy (1 Peter 1:16) and that he intends us to be partakers of his divine nature (2 Peter 1:4). It is therefore of extreme importance that we should understand not only what *holiness* means, but also how we become holy ourselves.

The meaning of holiness

As we examine the Old Testament we discover that there are four main aspects to the biblical concept of holiness or 'sanctification'. (The word 'sanctify' simply means 'to make holy' and in the original Hebrew and Greek of the Bible there is no distinction made between them).

First, holiness means *separation*. Genesis 2:3 says that God blessed the seventh day. 'Blessed' here means 'sanctified'. God set apart the seventh day. He separated it from the other days.

Secondly, holiness means *dedication*. God told the Israelites, 'Consecrate (sanctify) to me every firstborn' (Exodus 13:2). Every firstborn animal or child was dedicated to God. Thirdly, holiness means *purity.* In Exodus 19:10 the people were to be consecrated (sanctified) and were to *wash their clothes.* Similarly, in the New Testament, holiness is contrasted with uncleanness (1 Thessalonians 4:7).

Finally, holiness suggests *usefulness.* Aaron was consecrated in order that he might serve as a priest (Exodus 28:3). When God calls us to holiness, then, he is calling us to be separate from sin, dedicated completely to him, pure and clean that we might be useful in his service.

Already sanctified

Perhaps one of the greatest problems in understanding the doctrine of sanctification is that although God constantly challenges to be holy, he nevertheless repeatedly tells us that we are holy already! In the New Testament, Christians are generally referred to as *saints*, which means *holy ones.*

Paul could write to the church at Corinth (who were far from perfect Christians) describing them as those who 'have been and still are sanctified in Christ Jesus, called saints' (1 Corinthians 1:2, literal translation). They had once been thieves and drunkards, but now they were washed, they were sanctified, they were justified in the name of the Lord Jesus and by the Spirit of our God (1 Corinthians 6:11). This shows that their sanctification was something that had already taken place. In the context it is clear that this was at the same time as their justification – i.e. when they were converted.

Similarly Peter tells us that we are a holy nation (1 Peter 2:9), and Hebrews 10:10 declares that we have been sanctified through the offering of the body of Jesus Christ once and for all. There is, then, clearly a sense in which as Christians we have already been sanctified by virtue of Christ's death on Calvary and by virtue of our standing 'in Christ' as new-born sons of God.

Perfecting holiness

There is, however, another sense in which holiness has continually to be followed and put on, until it is established, perfected and completed. If our *status* in Christ is one of holiness, our *state*, in terms of every day practical living, may be rather different. Because, by virtue of Christ's death, God counts us as holy, we are encouraged to be holy in our actual conduct. To those who *are* a holy nation (1 Peter 2:9) God still says, '*Be* holy, because I am holy' (1 Peter 1:16).

Our sanctification is the revealed will of God. He has not called us to uncleanness, but to holiness. This involves keeping our bodies pure by abstaining from such things as sex outside marriage and dishonesty (1 Thessalonians 4:3-7). We are to make every effort to be holy because *without holiness no one will see the Lord* (Hebrews 12:14). We are to *put on the new self created to be like God in true righteousness and holiness* (Ephesians 4:24). Holiness must be perfected out of reverence for God (2 Corinthians 7:1).

As we *increase and overflow in love towards one another and towards all men* God will *strengthen our hearts so that we may be blameless and holy at the coming of the Lord Jesus* (1 Thessalonians 3:12-13). Paul's prayer for the Thessalonians was that God would sanctify them through and through (1 Thessalonians 5:23).

Just as we have been justified by faith in our Lord Jesus Christ, so too we have already been sanctified. God counts us as holy. But the outworking of that holiness must be seen in our living from day to day, and it is in that sense that our holiness has yet to be perfected. This completing of our sanctification is a gradual process throughout the life of the Christian believer, to be culminated in that great day when finally we shall be like him, for we shall see him as he is (1 John 3:2).

In the final analysis it is God alone who can make us holy, but that does not mean that we have no responsibility in the matter. Before turning our attention to the part we have to play, however, let us first consider the part God plays.

The part God plays

In fact God has already graciously done all that was necessary to make our sanctification possible. The finished work of Calvary is the sole grounds of our sanctification. Christ gave himself for us that we might be sanctified (Ephesians 5:25-26). He suffered so that we might be made holy through his blood (Hebrews 13:12). We are made holy through the offering of his body (Hebrews 10:10). He has reconciled us to God through his death on the cross in order to present us holy and without blemish and free from accusation (Colossians 1:22).

And yet he has gone even further. He has not only died for us, but he has raised us up to sit together with him in the heavenly realms (Ephesians 2:6) where he has blessed us with all spiritual blessings so that we would be *holy and blameless in his sight* (Ephesians 1:3-4). It is his wish that we should be sanctified through and through. He himself has promised to bring this about by the time of the coming of the Saviour (1 Thessalonians 5:23). The work of sanctification in our lives is brought about by the 'washing of the word' (Ephesians 5:26, c.f. John 17:17) and by the discipline of the Lord. We suffer hardship in order *that we may share in his holiness* (Hebrews 12:10).

The part we have to play

Despite God's promise to perfect the work of sanctification in our lives, however, there are certain responsibilities which we ourselves must face up to. First, we are to think differently. We are to be made new in the attitude of our minds (Ephesians 4:23). We are to count ourselves as dead to sin (Romans 6:11). We are to be transformed by the renewing of our mind (Romans 12:2). Our minds will be 'washed' with the word as we read it and meditate upon it. It is by God's promises that we purify ourselves (2 Corinthians 7:1). Our first responsibility, then, is to purify our minds with the word of God.

Secondly, we should remember Calvary. Hebrews 9:13 says, *If the blood of bulls and goats* (in the Old Testament) *sanctified... how much more will the blood of Christ cleanse our consciences...* Christ died that we might be sanctified. Let us remember his death, not only at communion, but let us be daily aware of the transforming power of his death for us.

Finally, there must be an active rejection of sin and a yielding of ourselves to righteousness. Ephesians 4:22-24 tells us that we are to 'put off the old self' (our old sinful nature) and 'put on the new self' (the new nature which we have received as a result of becoming a Christian). Before we became Christians we could not cease from sinning. We were powerless to help ourselves. But now we are born again. We are new creatures in Christ. We do sin sometimes, but we do not have to. We must think of ourselves differently. We must act differently. We must 'come out and be separate' and 'touch no unclean thing' (2 Corinthians 6:17). We must avoid sexual immorality (1 Thessalonians 4:3).

It is our responsibility to abstain from these things. It is our responsibility to 'increase in love' (1 Thessalonians 3:12), to *offer our bodies as living sacrifices, holy, and pleasing to God* (Romans 12:1), to offer our bodies 'in slavery to righteousness leading to holiness' (Romans 6:20). Once we were the slaves of sin (Romans 6:20). But now we have been set free, and have become, voluntarily, slaves to God. The benefit we reap leads to holiness, and the result is eternal life (Romans 6:22).

QUESTIONS

1. READ 1 Peter 1:16, 2 Peter 1:4

   What are we to be and why?

   What does God intend us to share?

2. READ 1 Peter 2:9, 1 Peter 1:16

   To what sort of nation is Peter writing?

   What does he encourage them to be?

3. READ Hebrews 9:14, 10:10

   What is it that cleanses us, and from what?

   What has made us holy?

   Will this ever need to be repeated?

4. READ 1 Thessalonians 3:12-13, 5:23

   As we increase and abound in love, what will the Lord do?

   What was Paul's prayer for these people?

5. READ Ephesians 5:25-26, Colossians 1:22

   What was the purpose of Christ's death on the cross?

6. READ Ephesians 1:3-4

   Why has God blessed us with every spiritual blessing in the heavenly realms?

7. READ Romans 6:11, 12:2, Ephesians 4:23

   What words are used in these verses to show us that we should think differently?

8. READ Ephesians 4:22-32

   What are we to do with our old self?

   What does this mean in practical terms?

CHAPTER TWENTY

Heaven and Hell

In our final chapter we turn our attention to what in some ways is the most puzzling mystery of life. People everywhere and in every age have sought to interpret it. To a great extent the existence of most of the world's major religions is a result of man's attempt to understand it. It is a universal phenomenon. We call it death.

As we saw right at the beginning of this book, what we believe is of vital importance. As we now turn in conclusion to the subject of life after death, the need for right teaching should be obvious to each one of us. How grateful we should be that, amid the dreadful darkness of the demonic doctrines propounded by the spiritists and by the heathen world in general, we have the searchlight of the word of God, breaking through the misty gropings of human imagination and speculation, illuminating our thinking, enlightening our minds and revealing the truth!

Not that the heathen world has possessed a monopoly of human speculation! The so-called Christian church has had its share! There is no biblical support for the doctrine of purgatory, or the teaching of universalism, or the belief in conditional immortality, soul-sleep and annihilation, for example. Whatever our background may be, if as born-again Christians we will search the scriptures with open hearts and with the help of the Holy Spirit, there are certain basic truths which, despite all difficulties, will stand out so clearly that only blind prejudice could possibly ever cause us to close our eyes to them.

The immortality of the soul

One fact about which both Old and New Testaments are extremely clear is that physical death is not the termination of our existence. The great emphasis, however, is not so much upon the immortality of the soul as upon the certainty of bodily resurrection. Nevertheless, continuity of existence after death is taught in the scriptures, and all theories of 'soul-sleep' must accordingly be rejected.

Even in the Old Testament man is not seen as ceasing to exist after death. His soul descends to 'Sheol' (usually translated 'grave' or 'hell') where the dead are gathered in tribes (Ezekiel 32:17-32) and receive the dying (Isaiah 14:9-10). It is in the New Testament, however, that the teaching is made explicit. In Matthew 22:32 the Lord Jesus made clear to the doubting Sadducees not only that Abraham, Isaac, and Jacob would one day rise from the dead, but that they were even 'living' at that very moment. To the repentant thief on the cross Jesus said, *Today you will be with me in paradise* (Luke 23:43).

Some have suggested that the story of the rich man and Lazarus (Luke 16:19-31) is simply a case of Jesus using current Jewish thought and not intended to be taken literally. But if that were so Jesus' teaching would be extremely misleading, to say the least! The literal truth of Jesus' words is confirmed by the apostle Peter who speaks of the unrighteous dead as 'spirits in prison' (1 Peter 3:19) and by the apostle Paul for whom to be 'away from the body' was to be 'at home with the Lord' (2 Corinthians 5:8).

The resurrection of the body

As we have already mentioned, however, a far greater emphasis is placed in scripture upon the certainty of physical resurrection for all mankind. What was foreseen by Isaiah (26:19) and Daniel (12:2), Jesus categorically stated:

A time is coming when all who are in the graves will hear his voice and come out; those who have done good will rise to live; and those who have done evil will rise to be condemned (John 5:28-29).

Compare also such passages as John 6:39, 40, 44; 11:24-25; 1 Corinthians 15:50-56, 1 Thessalonians 4:13-17; Revelation 20:13.

In the verses quoted above, and in Daniel 12:2, two different kinds of resurrection are clearly anticipated. Revelation 20:5-6 indicates that there is to be a time lapse of a thousand years between them. This is usually referred to as the *millennium*. The precise timing of such events related to the Second Coming of Christ need not concern us in this study, however. Equally sincere Christians hold a variety of differing views concerning this vastly complex subject. What is most important to notice is that all people are to be resurrected, some to life and others to condemnation. The really crucial question is, *Who goes where?*

Heaven and hell: who goes where?

As we have already seen in previous chapters, no one ever enters heaven by virtue of their own merit. All have sinned and come short of the glory of God (Romans 3:23). The end-product of sin is death (James 1:15, Romans 6:23). Our only hope is that God, who does not want anyone to perish (2 Peter 3:9), should have mercy on us. That mercy has in fact been demonstrated to us very clearly in that *while we were still sinners Christ died for us* (Romans 5:8).

It is God's revealed will that all people should be saved and come to the knowledge of the truth. This is why the Lord Jesus Christ, who is the only mediator between God and man, gave himself as a ransom for all (1 Timothy 2:3-6). John's Gospel makes it very clear that all those who put their trust in Christ's atoning sacrifice have everlasting life and that all others will be condemned (John 3:14-18, 36; 5:24; 6:47; 20:31).

The 'resurrection to life', then, is for those who have put their trust in Christ as Saviour. The 'resurrection to condemnation' is for those whom reject him. 2 Thessalonians 1:7-9 reveals that the essential nature of what we call 'hell' is *being shut out from the presence of the Lord.* Perhaps the simplest way to understand heaven and hell, then, is to think of heaven as eternity spent in God's presence and to think of hell as eternity shut off from God's presence.

In making this simplification, however, we must be careful not to minimise the awfulness of hell on the one hand or the glories of heaven on the other. The biblical descriptions of the torment of hell are extremely graphic and must never be taken lightly. It was Jesus himself who spoke of the fire of hell

(Matthew 5:22), outer darkness where there will be weeping and gnashing of teeth (Matthew 8:12) and eternal punishment (Matthew 25:46). It was Jesus who told us of a man tormented in hell (Luke 16:23). We should let the awful solemnity of these statements sink deep into our souls. Hell is revealed as everlasting, conscious punishment, and it is for those who will not believe (Mark 16:16).

The urgent need for action

As we meditate upon these divinely revealed truths we should pray that they may be indelibly impressed upon our hearts by the Spirit of God. God is not willing that any should perish. It is man who has determined his own destiny by his wilful rejection of God's love. God has done all that he can do to reconcile the sinner to himself. The work was finished at Calvary. Life is offered to all. For those who refuse God's offer of mercy the consequences are inevitable. For those who accept it there is the assurance of eternal life in heaven.

But all over the world there are still multitudes who have never really heard of God's love. Many are seeking to justify themselves in God's sight by their own futile efforts. They do not know that it is with the heart that you believe and are justified (Romans 10:10). They do not know that all they have to do is to call on the name of the Lord to be saved (Romans 10:13). *How then can they call on one whom they have not believed in? And how can they believe in the one of whom they have not heard? And how can they hear without someone preaching to them?* (Romans 10:14).

They cannot call on God to save them if they have not heard the good news of the gospel. And they will not hear unless they are told. And they will not be told unless we tell them. It is our responsibility to go into all the world to preach the gospel, to make disciples of all nations (Mark 16:15, Matthew 28:19). If we are going to do it effectively we will need to be endued with power from on high (Luke 24:49, Acts 1:8). But once we have been filled with the Spirit, it is our responsibility to go. If we really believe these things, we do well to ask ourselves what we are doing about it.

QUESTIONS

1. READ Matthew 22:32

   When Jesus said this, were Abraham, Isaac and Jacob still living on earth?

2. READ Luke 23:43

   Would this man go on living?

3. READ 2 Corinthians 5:8

   What would it mean for Paul to be 'absent from the body'?

4. READ John 5:28-29, Revelation 20:4-6

   What two kinds of resurrection are mentioned?

   What time lapse will there be between them?

5. READ 2 Peter 3:19, 1 Timothy 2:3-6

   What is God not willing for?

   What is God's will?

6. READ John 3:14-18, 36; 5:24; 20:31

   Does this leave any doubt that all who trust in Christ have everlasting life?

   Does this leave any doubt that all others will be condemned?

7. READ 2 Thessalonians 1:7-9

   How do these verses reveal the essential nature of hell?

8. READ Romans 10:9-14

   How do these verses stress our responsibility to share the gospel with others?

Also by David Petts:

THE HOLY SPIRIT – an introduction

In this clearly written and easily readable book Dr David Petts answers questions like:

Who is the Holy Spirit? How can I answer the Jehovah's Witnesses who say that the Holy Spirit is only an impersonal force? Should we worship the Holy Spirit? What is our answer to those who deny the Virgin Birth? What is the blasphemy against the Holy Spirit? How can I help someone who believes they have committed the unforgivable sin? What role does the Spirit play in the work of conversion? Can the Holy Spirit help me live a holy life? What is the Baptism in the Holy Spirit? How do I know if I've received it? How can I receive and maintain the fulness of the Spirit? Do I have to be baptized in the Spirit to manifest the fruit of the Spirit? What are the gifts of the Spirit and how can I receive them and use them? What's the role of the Holy Spirit in the life of the church? What's the connection between the Holy Spirit and the age to come?

Written from a distinctly charismatic perspective this book will both inform you and inspire you. The author's balanced approach, with his insistence that our experience of the Spirit must be understood and evaluated in the light of biblical revelation, gives the reader confidence that the writer is familiar with the Holy Spirit's work not only from his study of the Word of God but also from personal experience.

Published by Mattersey Hall for £6.99   €10.99 $10.99

Available from the author:

www.davidpetts.org

Body Builders – Gifts to Make God's People Grow

The Christian Church is growing faster today than at any time since the early days of the first apostles. Despite the attention drawn by the media to dwindling congregations in some places, in many countries the good news about Jesus is spreading rapidly. One of the main reasons for this is the renewed emphasis that is being placed on the supernatural gifts of the Holy Spirit, so that the gospel is not only preached, but confirmed by amazing signs and wonders.

In Part One of this exciting and easily readable book, Dr David Petts gives clear teaching on the role of apostles, prophets, evangelists, pastors and teachers in the Church today. All five of these Ephesians 4:11 ministries are needed for the Church, the body of Christ, to be built up.

In Part Two he deals with the supernatural gifts that the Holy Spirit gives to Christians in order to make God's people grow. He explains what they are and how they may be received and used today. Although firmly based on the teaching of the New Testament, the book contains numerous inspiring illustrations from the author's personal experience of God's miracle-working power.

Published by Mattersey Hall

Available from the author:

www.davidpetts.org

First edition 2002, 280pp.

£9.99   US$14.99   €14.99

Just a Taste of Heaven – a biblical and balanced approach to God's healing power

In this easily readable book Dr David Petts shows clearly why we should expect miracles of healing today. He looks at most of the healing miracles in the Bible and draws important lessons from them.

He offers a balanced theology of healing that seeks to promote faith for healing without causing discouragement to those who are not healed.

Using illustrations from his own experience he gives wise advice on how healing should be practised both in evangelism and in pastoral ministry today.

Published by Mattersey Hall

Available from the author:

www.davidpetts.org

£9.99   €15.99   US$15.99

ISBN   1-873324-08-1

How to Live for Jesus

How to Live for Jesus is a clear, simple and practical guide on how to live the Christian life. It is intended primarily for those who have just come to faith in Christ and may be studied individually or in a group setting. Its ten chapters are based on a series of talks given by the author to young converts in churches he has pastored.

Available from the author:

www.davidpetts.org

44pp. Individual copies £3.00 each.

Substantial discounts are given for churches ordering 10 copies or more. Please enquire via the website.